Craig Groeschel digs his heels in and actually names all those pesky behaviors that so often get us into trouble. Don't read *Soul Detox* without a sturdy pair of steel-toed boots, because Craig isn't afraid to step on your toes.

— DAVE RAMSEY, *New York Times* bestselling author; nationally syndicated radio host

In every generation, God sends a few voices to boldly speak his truth to a world that desperately needs him. Pastor Craig Groeschel is one of those voices for our generation. As the pastor to one of the largest churches in America, his wisdom and insight are unparalleled. So when he challenges us to consider a new perspective on how God's Word informs our lives, we need to listen. In *Soul Detox*, you will learn from a man who has earned the right to speak through his personal integrity and leadership in the body of Christ. So prepare yourself to embrace God's purpose for your life by letting go of toxic sins that are holding you back.

— STEVEN FURTICK, Lead Pastor, Elevation Church; author, *Sun Stand Still*

To be holy and transformed into the image of Jesus, we all need a regular soul detox. When we allow his light to shine into our darkness, healing and wholeness come. A timely message for our generation.

— CHRISTINE CAINE, Founder, The A21 Campaign

Craig Groeschel shines a light on those dark, secret corners of our spiritual lives that we'd probably rather just ignore. He pinpoints widespread virulent cultural influences that corrode the soul and tarnish our relationship with God. Read *Soul Detox* and gain powerful tools essential for stripping away that cultural grime and reclaiming God's greatest desires for our lives.

— ANDY STANLEY, North Point Community Church

Every generation faces its own set of challenges. People today seem to be especially broken and hurting. But the good news is that Jesus is the answer to every generation's problems. Craig Groeschel does an excellent job of teaching how broken people can find hope and healing in the midst of today's challenges. I have great respect for Craig as a thinker and leader, and I recommend this book.

— JOHN C. MAXWELL, *New York Times* bestselling author; leadership expert

With the frank honesty, trademark humor, and biblical insight that we've come to expect from Craig Groeschel, *Soul Detox* challenges us to live counterculturally. Bravely, Craig invites us to strike the delicate balance of living in the world without being conformed to its steadily declining moral standards. His words challenge us to live in a radical way that glorifies God and preserves his transformative work in us. Every page will bring conviction and then, with great care, offer grace and instruction on how to move forward victoriously. The change you may have been looking for will begin in these pages. Read on and be blessed.

— PRISCILLA SHIRER, Bible teacher; author

Craig has that glow about him that you wish you had. Then you realize it's because of a committed discipline of spirit, soul, and body that he has cultivated in his life, family, and ministry. Its contagious nature calls you to pursue the same process of detox and maintenance. This book will enable all who read to attain the same result.

— ISRAEL HOUGHTON, worship leader; songwriter

Most people who are hurting are doing so on a much deeper level than they realize, and only through looking deep inside their souls and going through a detox can they find healing and the abundant life that Jesus offers. I am so glad that Craig wrote this book because, in my opinion, he is one of the best teachers on the planet in regard to taking the Scriptures and helping people see their lives through them.

— PERRY NOBLE, Senior Pastor, NewSpring Church

Every preacher tells you what is wrong with murder and adultery. In *Soul Detox*, Groeschel dares to tackle comfortable Christian sins such as gossip, materialism, and fear. You won't put this book down feeling condemned; rather you will be encouraged with the tools you need to come clean.

— TIM STEVENS, Executive Pastor, Granger Community Church;
author, *Pop Goes the Church*

Soul Detox is a must-read if you want to do a checkup on your behaviors, emotions, and all that influences your life. This book will help you detox from the stuff that poisons you and causes damage to your relationships and ministry. Read this book before it is too late!

— DAVE FERGUSON, Lead Pastor, Community Christian Church; spiritual entrepreneur, NewThing

I am thankful for Craig Groeschel's honest, humorous, and soul-convicting voice in my life and in our world. This is a relevant ethics book for our "now" generation that will stir souls and sift out excuses, ignorance, and influences that hold us hostage from God's best for our lives.

— DINO RIZZO, Lead Pastor, Healing Place Church

All too often I've heard it said that pastors of large churches have a soft message, but in this book, Craig Groeschel, who leads one of America's largest churches, strongly calls his readers to repentance. Since soft words produce hard people and hard words produce soft people, Pastor Craig's difficult challenge to his readers to reflect on toxins in their souls that are poisoning their holiness is a welcome addition in an evangelical culture that minimizes sin and offers cheap grace.

— MARK DRISCOLL, Founder and Preaching Pastor, Mars Hill Church

Craig Groeschel has written a powerful and timely prescription for the most devastating ailment in modern society: neglect of the soul. I love how Craig speaks from his heart and lays out a practical, biblical treatment plan that will nourish your soul to health and change your life!

— KERRY SHOOK, coauthor, *New York Times* bestselling *One Month to Live* and *Love at Last Sight*; Senior Pastor, Woodlands Church

Craig Groeschel is one of the most inspirational leaders in the body of Christ. His powerful new book will empower you to live the abundant life Christ has for you. *Soul Detox* will change you inside out, freeing you from guilt, fear, worry, and condemnation.

— JENTEZEN FRANKLIN, Senior Pastor, Free Chapel; author, *New York Times* bestselling *Fasting*

Craig Groeschel inspires me to *want* to grow in my faith. In *Soul Detox*, he offers a compelling and clear look at what it means to live as a Christian in today's complex world. With honesty, humor, and profound insight, these pages will lead you closer to Jesus.

— JUD WILHITE, author, *Torn*; Senior Pastor,
Central Christian Church

As I did when reading Craig's other writings, I laughed and cried at his stories, but *Soul Detox* goes a layer deeper. It's his genuine honesty and biblical advice you'll remember. It's a spiritual cleanse in literary form. My soul needed this book; I suspect yours might too.

— DAVE STONE, Pastor, Southeast Christian Church

Every once in a while, we all need a "soul detox." All of us need to remove what Craig Groeschel calls the seeds of poison that infiltrate our hearts and lives. *Soul Detox* will help you search for, identify, and remedy detrimental emotions, moods, attitudes, and actions that cause us so much frustration and confusion as Christians. With an emphasis on internal examination lived out through external relationships, *Soul Detox* is a great read for anyone who wants to live a fulfilled Christian life.

— TODD RHOADES, blog writer, *ToddRhoades.com*;
Director, Leadership Network

If you are weary of the worldly, watered-down, waste-of-time experience that so many people in the North American church live, I commend this book to you. We will never experience God's glory — that is, the evidence that God has been somewhere — until we start living in purity according to God's Word.

— DR. JAMES MACDONALD, Senior Pastor, Harvest Bible Church

Craig masterfully shows us how to clear the clutter in our minds that keeps us from our true potential. You're going to love this book!

— BIL CORNELIUS, Pastor, Bay Area Fellowship; author,
bestselling *I Dare You to Change*

SOUL DETOX

Clean Living in a Contaminated World

CRAIG GROESCHEL

ZONDERVAN.com/
AUTHORTRACKER
follow your favorite authors

We want to hear from you. Please send your comments about this book to us in care of zreview@zondervan.com. Thank you.

ZONDERVAN

Soul Detox
Copyright © 2012 by Craig Groeschel

This title is also available as a Zondervan ebook. Visit www.zondervan.com/ebooks.

This title is also available in a Zondervan audio edition.
Visit www.zondervan.fm.

Requests for information should be addressed to:

Zondervan, *Grand Rapids, Michigan 49530*

Library of Congress Cataloging-in-Publication Data

Groeschel, Craig.
    Soul detox : pure living in a polluted world / Craig Groeschel.
      p. cm.
    ISBN 978-0-310-33368-5 (hardcover) 1. Christian life. I. Title.
    BV4501.3.G756 2012
    248.4—dc23   2011036687

Cover design: Curt Diepenhorst
Cover photography: Jeffrey Coolidge / Getty Images®
Interior design: Katherine Lloyd, The DESK

Printed in the United States of America

---

13 14 15 16 /DCI/ 26 25 24 23 22 21 20 19 18 17 16 15 14 13 12 11 10 9 8 7 6 5 4 3

Dear friends, I warn you as
"temporary residents and foreigners" to keep
away from worldly desires that wage war
against your very souls.

— 1 Peter 2:11 NLT

Contents

Part 3

TOXIC INFLUENCES

Coming Clean

God doesn't seek for golden vessels, and does not ask
for silver ones, but He must have clean ones.
—Dwight L. Moody

When I was growing up, it seemed like all grown-ups smoked, all the moms continually twirling Virginia Slims between their fingers while the dads talked with a Marlboro or Camel dangling from the corner of their mouths. They all enjoyed their cigarettes, which I gathered were probably better than what most of them smoked in the '60s. My own mom and dad, although wonderful parents in too many ways to count, fit right in with their peers and smoked at least two packs a day.

Being raised in a house filled with smoke, I was never bothered by the smell. A nonsmoking guest would have instantly identified it and likely complained, but my family thought nothing of it. Most of us probably have a smell we associate with growing up — our mom's pine cleaner or our dad's Old Spice. For me the smell was cigarette smoke. I found it strangely comforting because it was what made home smell like home.

Since all my buddies' parents also smoked, their homes had the same odor — all except for Mike's house. Although I didn't know why at the time, I remember loving the way Mike's home smelled. Each time I walked in the front door, I felt like I'd just entered a Sea Breeze commercial. It's hard to describe what "clean" smells like, but I thought Mike's mom knew the secret formula. Not only did every room sparkle, but they smelled so fresh, lemony, and bright, as if his mom had just finished dusting with Pledge before we walked in. Looking back, I know that the fresh, cool smell wasn't just the presence of air freshener but the absence of cigarette smoke. No one lit up at Mike's house.

While the health risks of smoking were well known at the time, it was a few years before the American Medical Association came out with its findings on the dangers of secondhand smoke, especially for children. Their conclusions led to a series of public service announcements that showed toddlers lighting up and puffing away and other similarly shocking scenes. No one's parents were trying to poison their family and cause health problems. Nonetheless, they unknowingly put all the people they loved — including themselves — at risk.

Where There's Smoke

It seems funny to me now in a sad, ironic kind of way. Parents of all shapes and sizes lovingly warned their children: "Look both ways before you cross the street." "Put on your coat so you don't catch a cold." "Wash your hands so you don't get sick." "Don't get in the water until thirty minutes after you've eaten." (I still don't get that one.) Though they did everything within their power to keep us safe and protect us from harm's way, many parents were unknowingly poisoning their kids with secondhand smoke.

I didn't realize how unhealthy my home was until I got outside it enough to breathe freely and experience the difference. In fact, after living in a smoke-free environment for the first time ever in my college dorm, when I returned home, I was shocked.

The walls, which I remembered as a crisp white, held a dull, yellowish tint. A pale gray film coated the air. Even when no one had a cigarette lit, an unmistakable haze filled the room and enveloped us all. And as soon as I walked in the door, the odor slapped me in the face. Instead of having the comfortable and familiar smell of my home, my old dwelling place smelled like a stale ashtray.

Upon my return to school, my roommate "Spiff" grimaced when I walked into our dorm room. Clearly, my clothes and duffel bag carried the musty smell of cigarette smoke. "You're rank!" he shouted before throwing my bag in the hallway and telling me to shower.

My stomach sank as it dawned on me. For the first eighteen years of my life, I lived in a cloud of secondhand smoke, oblivious to how it was coating my skin, my lungs, my throat. Not only did I smell like a chimney, but I unknowingly inhaled poison on a daily basis. I didn't blame my parents; they didn't know that secondhand smoke is practically as dangerous as inhaling it firsthand. But their ignorance didn't change the reality of the situation.

Spiritual Pollution

I'm proud to say that both my parents overcame their addiction to tobacco and did what many seem unable to do — quit smoking. They recognized that something they enjoyed and accepted had the potential to harm themselves and those they loved most.

I'm convinced that many of us are living in this same kind of dangerous trap with our spiritual health. We know something doesn't feel quite right, that we're not growing closer to God and following Christ the way we would like, but we can't put our finger on it. Even though we believe in God and want to please him, we find it hard to serve him passionately and consistently. We want to move forward spiritually but feel like we're running against the wind. We want more — we know there's more — but we just can't seem to find it.

Why do so many well-meaning Christians take one spiritual step forward, then slide back two? Why do we long for more of God in our lives and yet feel farther and farther away from him? What's holding us back from growing in this relationship that we claim is our main priority?

While many factors go into answering these questions, ultimately I believe our spiritual enemy blinds us with a smoke screen of poisonous distractions. Just like I lived unaware of the smoke in my home, many people aren't fully aware of the forces stunting their spiritual growth. Without realizing the impact on their faith, people embrace harmful relationships, consume toxic media, live with addictive habits, and remain oblivious to the long-term effects. We think the way we live is perfectly fine, normal, harmless, or even positive. Some people don't want to take an honest look at the way they live, claim-ing, "What you don't know won't hurt you."

Unfortunately, this just isn't true. Many individuals who inhaled secondhand smoke — not to mention all the millions of smokers — have suffered permanent and painful physical effects. The truth is this: what many people don't know is not just hurting them but killing them spiritually.

You've probably heard that if you put a frog in a kettle of water and heat the water slowly to a boil, the frog will adjust to the warm-ing water and won't even realize that it's boiling to death. How is this possible? The increase in temperature is so graduated that what feels like a warm bath at first becomes a hot tub before kicking into double-boiler mode. By that time, it's too late. The frog's body adjusts to his surroundings, never noticing that what surrounds him is draining the life out of him.

In our culture, the water temperature increases daily. Without real-izing it, we slowly become acclimated to a toxic environment full of poi-sonous influences. As the water temperature rises, we keep pretending we're soaking in a hot tub having the time of our lives, never dreaming that we're scalding our souls. As we become scarred and desensitized to what is right and wrong, good and evil, life-giving and life-draining, we lose sight of our first love. We move away from God one degree at a time.

The Devil's Advocate

I know firsthand how this process works. Several years after becom-ing a Christian, I reflected on all the parts of my life that God had changed. Rather than occasionally telling other people what I thought they wanted to hear — I believe that's called *lying* — I allowed God to make me a person of truth. Instead of sharing the latest rumors about mutual friends with others — I think that's called *gossiping* — I learned to hold my tongue. While I used to criticize people freely without regard for their feelings or the situation (my old friend *self-righteousness*), I learned to discern a loving response. Although many of my old ways changed after I gave my life to Christ, my movie-viewing habits didn't.

My wife, Amy, and I had been married several years when she expressed her concern about the kinds of movies we watched. One evening while we were talking, she gently asked, "Do you really think the movies we're watching are honoring to God?"

"It's not like we're watching porn!" I shot back, offended by her implied accusation. "There's nothing wrong with enjoying a little entertainment." Without giving her time to load up on ammunition by citing the last few movies we'd seen, I tried to make a preemptive strike. "Besides, some violence, bad language, and a little sex scene here and there doesn't really bother me. I'm more than mature enough to handle it." Perfect — I could make this her problem and not mine!

I'd used that same defense countless times. However, when I heard myself shift into my default setting, the words didn't sound as convincing as they once had. My wife let it go, but her question remained with me.

A couple of nights later, we met two of our best friends, Scott and Shannon, for dinner and a movie. All through the meal, we discussed our spiritual growth with lots of God talk. Shannon was learning more about serving God in her daily life. Scott continued to enjoy the blessings of God in his insurance business. Amy talked nonstop about what God was teaching her through her time in the Word. And I talked freely about all the people coming to know Christ through our church. After our thanksgiving-filled dinner, we bought tickets for *The Devil's Advocate,* a must-see thriller that some friends had recommended.

A few minutes into the movie, the peace, encouragement, and gratitude I'd enjoyed at dinner disappeared. Onscreen violence, bad language, and sexual content that had never bothered me before started to get under my skin. I internally cringed when each F-bomb landed or God's name was taken in vain. Before long, two women caressed each other. By the end of the movie, we had endured an extended scene in which a ghost explicitly rapes a woman.

We all felt sickened.

I later apologized to Amy. Her loving words stung because I didn't want to hear them, but they were true. Like the frog in the kettle, I'd become acclimated. Just because something didn't bother me didn't mean that it wasn't having a negative impact. In fact, what did it say about me that filthy language, brutal violence, and explicit sex on the screen didn't bother me? How had my standards, instead of God's standards, become the norm?

Now, I don't believe we should draw a line in the cultural sand and live in a sanitized little bubble. On the other hand, we can't just immerse ourselves in every aspect of the world around us and let culture determine our lifestyle habits indiscriminately. Most filmmakers aren't worrying about the impact of their movie on your soul. Most pop songs on iTunes don't care whether they build up your faith or draw you closer to God. It is our responsibility to discern what we let into our lives and what we keep out.

If you're a Christian, wouldn't you agree that there has to be a line of right and wrong somewhere? A way to discern what pleases God and moves us closer to him instead of farther away? And can we trust our own sensibilities to know what's truly best for us?

Could it be that we've become desensitized to what is right or wrong, good or evil, pleasing or displeasing to our holy God? Is it possible that what we consider normal entertainment could be dangerous to our souls? Do you think that what we consider laughable, entertaining, or simply fun, God might find heartbreaking?

For those of us who follow Jesus, everything we do, no matter where we go, should reflect our love and commitment to him. God is with us just as much when we're in a dark movie theater laughing at F-bombs from comedic characters as he is when we're in church singing in the choir.

Everything counts.

Everything that we allow into our minds, hearts, and lives — everything that we spend our time and money on — has an impact on how we grow, or don't grow, spiritually. As the old computer adage reminds us: garbage in, garbage out. Just as we are what we eat physically, we are also what we consume spiritually. If we don't monitor and adjust our diet accordingly, our souls are in danger of absorbing more and more lethal poison.

Muddy Waters

The Bible consistently reminds us to check our spiritual diet for toxins. Proverbs 25:26 says, "Like a muddied spring or a polluted well are the righteous who give way to the wicked." How muddy is your water right now? Is your well polluted by all the cultural toxins seeping in? Or does your spiritual well draw on Living Water as its pure, thirst-quenching source? Maybe you're a Christian — you've been made righteous by Christ — yet you've become a muddied spring or a polluted well, and you don't even know it.

You might believe, "My thoughts don't matter. As long as they stay tucked away inside my head, they're not hurting anyone. We all think about things that we'd never do, right?" All the while your negative thoughts are silently poisoning your soul, pouring lies into your spiritual water supply. Unfortunately, our thoughts don't just stay in our head, disconnected from our words and our actions. Unhealthy thoughts often lead to unhealthy words. Without even knowing it, you might be talking yourself, and others, out of God's best.

Or maybe it's the people that you hang with regularly. You know they aren't full-on for God, but no big deal. You don't want them to think you're some kind of religious freak or anything. So you keep doing whatever they do, going wherever they go. Though you believe one thing, you live a totally different way.

Maybe you've resigned yourself to certain struggles in your life — anger, lust, discontentment — as nothing more than your personal quirks. "It's just the way I am," you tell yourself, all the while your spiritual enemy laughs at the cancer you continue to feed in your soul.

Rather than experiencing the richness of a dynamic, intimate relationship with the righteous One, you put God in a little box that you can check off your to-do list each week. By settling for rules and religion and feeling pretty good about how much you're doing for the church and those less fortunate, you become blinded to legalism and self-righteousness.

It's time to come clean.

If you're tired of the stain of sinful habits discoloring your life, if you long to breathe the fresh, clean, life-giving air of God's holiness, if you would love to detoxify your soul from guilt, fear, regret, and all the impurities that pollute your relationship with God, then this book is for you. In the pages that follow, we'll examine the various pollutants that often corrupt our spiritual desire to know and serve God. Some can be avoided as we become more discerning and remove them from our surroundings. Others may linger like smoke in the air but can be managed in ways that will alleviate their impact.

My prayer is that what you read will push you, challenge you, and at times even make you mad. If you're aware of the truth, then you should be upset, because you've been breathing smoke-polluted thoughts, life-draining words, and sin-filled actions without realizing the toll they're taking on your relationship with God. Deep down, you know there's a truer way to live, a deeper, purer way to love, and a larger impact to make on the world around you. It's time to open your eyes, your heart, and your mind to the cleansing power of God's truth.

His Word is filled with stories of men and women who needed

to come clean, who longed for more. One of my favorites is David, who's described as "a man after God's own heart" but, as you may know, was far from perfect. Shortly after he committed adultery and murder, David experienced a soul sickness that affected him on every level — physical, emotional, and spiritual. He knew his sins of lust, entitlement, and deception were killing his heart. He knew the only way to be restored and experience a joyful, fulfilling life again was to come clean before God. In his prayer of repentance, he wrote,

> Wash away all my iniquity
> and cleanse me from my sin.
> Cleanse me with hyssop, and I will be clean;
> wash me, and I will be whiter than snow.
> Create in me a pure heart, O God,
> and renew a steadfast spirit within me.
> Restore to me the joy of your salvation
> and grant me a willing spirit, to sustain me.
>
> — Psalm 51:2, 7, 10, 12

Wouldn't you like to come clean? To feel your Father's love wash over you like the cool, crystal waters of a spring-fed stream? To leave the smoke-filled room where you've been hiding and come into his life-giving light? To breathe in fresh spiritual air?

It's not too late.

If you want to detoxify your soul and renew your faith, if you want more from your relationship with God, then turn the page.

Part 1

TOXIC BEHAVIORS

1

Deception Infection

Telling Ourselves the Truth

The ingenuity of self-deception is inexhaustible.

—Hannah Moore

As a pastor, I rarely confess to watching *American Idol*, since it sounds kind of ... idolatrous. Nevertheless, I've been known to catch a few weeks each season (or maybe all of them, but who's counting?). My favorites are the first few shows as the panel travels around the country for auditions. If you don't believe people are easily self-deceived, you only have to watch these tryouts to change your mind. It's difficult to comprehend how many horrifically bad singers truly believe they deserve to be the next vocal superstar!

While we often laugh (or cringe, if you're more compassionate than I am) and wonder how a person can be so out of touch with reality, so unaware of their utter lack of talent, I'm afraid I actually understand their problem. You see, I have another confession to share with you, one that I'm even more embarrassed to disclose. Growing up, I not only loved to sing, but I thought I was a *great* singer. I'd wail out "You Ain't Nothin' but a Hound Dog" or "(I Can't Get No) Satisfaction" at the top of my lungs, convinced that it was only a matter of time before I was discovered. Holding my invisible microphone, I'd shake my hips like Elvis, pout my lips like Mick Jagger, and snarl like Billy Idol. No wonder I sounded like a wounded animal!

Convinced of my future stardom, in the fifth grade I auditioned for our grade school choir. The choir consisted of fifty singers; fifty-two kids were trying out. Obviously, two unfortunate wannabes would not make the cut. I figured the odds were clearly stacked in my favor. This was my big chance to let others in on the secret talent that would make me a household name someday.

Yes, you are absolutely correct about what happened at the auditions. I was one of the two that went home crying because I didn't make the stupid choir! So each time I see some poor clueless young man or woman singing off-key on *Idol*, surprised at Randy Jackson's "That's enough, Dawg," it's easy for me to understand their self-deception. What's more challenging for me to understand is how their friends and family support and perpetuate their delusion. Those poor mothers making obscene gestures at the judges for not recognizing their baby's amazing vocal talent!

As we see ourselves through the lens of our experiences, beliefs, and perspectives, we all have our blind spots. As the Bible describes the problem, "The heart is deceitful above all things" (Jer. 17:9). No matter how objective we hope to be, our viewpoint is always distorted to some — sometimes large — degree. Here's the challenge. The longer we view ourselves through a distorted lens, the more likely we are to believe a distorted truth. The longer we lie to ourselves, deceive ourselves, or remain in denial about the truth, the more likely we are to base our decisions and actions on this false belief system.

Flattery Will Get You Somewhere

If you're like most people, when you read about self-deception, it's easy to think of a few people who fall into that category, but chances are that in your mind, *you* are not one of them. The reason is clear. We don't know what we don't know about ourselves. And often we don't *want* to know. I believe God put this book into your hands because he loves you so much, he wants to help show you anything in your life that is polluting his plan for you, including your shortcomings and the defenses you may be placing around them.

Since we see ourselves from only one perspective, it's incredibly difficult to get an accurate picture of ourselves. In order to see into our blind spots, we must use different mirrors held at different angles. I'd like to provide you with some of these mirrors in order to expose the toxic behaviors that tend to sneak up on all of us. They're often present on a daily basis, and even though we can't see them, they can accumulate inside us and poison the well of our souls.

Why can't we see our self-generated toxins? David answers this question in Psalm 36:2 – 3 when he describes a deceived sinner: "In their own eyes they *flatter themselves too much to detect or hate their sin*. The words of their mouths are wicked and deceitful; they fail to act wisely or do good" (emphasis mine). Notice how David puts it, that some people "flatter themselves too much." They lie to themselves and don't even know it. And they've become so skilled at self-deception that they cannot detect or confess their sins. Basically, we manufacture our own poison and administer regular doses to ourselves.

Chances are good you know someone like this. Perhaps you have a friend who gossips all the time. He says boastfully, "I don't gossip; I'm just telling you so you can pray for them." You and everyone else know he's a gossip. Or maybe you have a family member who is off-the-charts rude. Yet she would tell you, "I'm not trying to be offensive; I just tell it like it is." Odds are you know someone who has a drinking problem. Yet this person denies having any problem and adamantly believes he can quit at any time. You might have a friend who thinks he's God's gift to women, but you and everyone else know he's an arrogant, womanizing, self-centered jerk. You possibly work for a woman who thinks she's a great leader at the office, but everyone else knows that she is a micromanaging, overbearing, control freak. Why don't these people see it in themselves?

Recently at church I asked our congregation, "How many of you battle with self-deception?" A few people in the crowd raised their hands. Then I asked, "How many of you know someone who is very self-deceived?" You guessed it. Almost everyone knew someone else who's guilty of self-deception.

Chances are you do too. You probably know someone who thinks more highly of themselves than they should. Or you might have a relative who thinks he's funny, but everyone else thinks he's annoying. You likely know someone who has a problem but will deny it until the cows come home. It's hard to be objective about ourselves.

I laughed as I explained to our church that we have a statistical problem. Almost no one in our church believes that they are self-deceived, and yet almost everyone knows someone who is. Why? Because we have an unlimited capacity to deceive ourselves. As we lie to ourselves ("I'm a great singer"), we start to believe our lies. The more we tell the lies, the more we believe they are truth.

Before long, we wholeheartedly embrace a distorted reality skillfully created by a willed ignorance. We deny, suppress, or minimize what is true. By default, we assert, adorn, and elevate what is false. When we finally see the truth, we think the truth is a lie.

We could say it this way: those who don't know, don't know that they don't know. If you are deceived, chances are pretty good you don't know that you believe something untrue — otherwise you wouldn't be deceived. If we never identify the lies and replace them with truth, we'll forever crave a healthy life on a diet of poison and always wonder why we are sick.

Ticked Off

So how do we begin identifying our self-told lies and replacing them with truth? Through the process of ruthless self-examination. After my kids spend a long day playing in the woods, I always have them check themselves for ticks. They loathe this somewhat embarrassing self-examination since it requires them to go over every square inch of their bodies slowly and carefully. But they know that catching a tick early can keep them from getting seriously ill.

Similarly, I'd encourage you to do a thorough internal self-examination. Just as those pesky bloodsuckers jump on you when you enter their environment, spiritual toxins infuse your thinking as you wade through our culture. Take an honest look at the way you live, how you think, and who or what influences you the most. Work hard to be brutally honest.

Examine your life for toxic behaviors — anything you do that cripples your spiritual effectiveness or distracts you from your eternal mission. Look within for toxic emotions — any deep feelings that lead you away from God's truth. Take an honest look at any unhealthy consumptions — the media you consume, the sites you surf, the people you spend the most time around. The first step to defeating an enemy is to recognize your opponent. Though your enemy might be invisible, God can give you eyes to see.

Let me warn you, though. The closer you get to uncovering a toxic killer in your life, the harder your enemy will fight to keep his grip. If you are like me, you might even unknowingly betray yourself and fight against the change. Denial is often our first line of defense. We're skilled at taking responsibility for little and justifying much.

Be careful when you hear yourself think or utter these phrases or something similar:

- I don't have a problem with this.
- It's really no big deal. This is one way I cope with everything.
- I'm not as bad as most people.

- I can quit anytime I want to.
- This is just the way I am.

Those who are most defensive are often the most unknowingly guilty. It's been said that the more convinced you are that you're right, the more likely you are wrong. If you fight back against those trying to help you, chances are you are fighting to keep your own lies intact. If someone who loves you tries to show you a dangerous pattern in your life, you might be 100 percent convinced they are wrong when the truth is they are 100 percent correct.

Peter, in the New Testament, is a perfect example. When Jesus explained that some of the disciples would fall away and deny him, Peter was convinced that he never would. With unshakable confidence, Peter replied, "Even if all fall away on account of you, *I never will*" (Matt. 26:33, emphasis mine). Can you hear his self-deceived confidence?

As he flattered himself, Peter was unaware of his toxic self-deception. In the very next verse, we find Jesus explaining that before the rooster crows, Peter will deny Jesus three times. But Peter stood his ground and declared, "Even if I have to die with you, I will *never* disown you" (Matt. 26:35, emphasis mine). Sure enough, before the day ended, not one, not two, but — count 'em — *three* different times Peter denied even knowing who Jesus was.

If someone has been trying to show you something about yourself and you continue to fight it, maybe it's time to acknowledge that you might be deceived. Your spouse might be convinced you have a problem with painkillers or alcohol or another drug, but you stand your ground and say that you don't. Someone might have told you that you're addicted to video games or social media, but you don't believe it. Maybe several loved ones have told you that you are a workaholic, but you don't stop working to listen. If you find yourself resisting or fighting back, be careful. Those who are most convinced are often the most deceived. Be careful not to flatter yourself so much that you cannot detect or hate your own sin.

No Laughing Matter

Since it is hauntingly easy to deceive ourselves, we need outside help to become more objective about our blind spots. And if our shields are up and our defenses are operating at full force, we may not be hearing what those around us are saying. Sometimes if we really want to change, we must ask God to show us what's true about how we're thinking, talking, and living.

In my early years at our church, people complained to me regularly that I was being unnecessarily crude when I preached. To them, some of my illustrations and humor crossed the line of what's appropriate. I told myself that they were just being prudish and didn't understand my sense of humor and strategy.

Though more people complained, I stood my ground. After all, if they had known me before I was a Christian, they'd be blown away by how much I'd improved. Besides, my slightly off-color humor was connecting with unchurched people, men and women visiting our church for the first time. I couldn't help it if these other "legalistic" people didn't have the freedom that I enjoyed.

Many of our church's most faithful leaders set up meeting after meeting to talk to me about my "problem." To be honest, I was growing weary of their incessant complaints. They just weren't as evangelistic as I was and obviously didn't have a good sense of humor. At the end of what seemed like the hundredth meeting about my jokes, an exceptionally wise older gentleman asked me to pray. "Since you're convinced you're not doing anything wrong," he continued sincerely, "would you ask God to show you if he would have you change?" Just to get this guy off my back, I reluctantly agreed to pray, although I knew it wouldn't change my stance.

Not wanting to break my word, a few days later I half-heartedly prayed something like, "God, I know all these people are wrong, but if there is something you need to show me about cleaning up my act, please do."

Be careful what you pray for.

The very next Sunday, my oldest daughter, Catie, who was seven at the time, came to "big church" and sat with my wife, Amy, while I preached. I glanced at my innocent daughter, smiling attentively and holding her Precious Moments Bible proudly in its pink case. Right as I was about to begin with a colorful joke, I hesitated. In one sweeping moment, God showed me clearly. I had been crude.

When I was about to say something that was truly funny but not totally clean, I realized that I wouldn't want my seven-year-old daughter saying the very phrase I was about to say while preaching. In fact, if I heard her say the words that I was about to say, I'd correct her and tell her it wasn't appropriate.

Busted.

If I don't want my daughter telling this joke, why should I?

For so long, I had been blind to my toxic words and risqué humor. All along I thought I was funny and reaching people who normally didn't go to church. Even when I was convinced my method was solid, everyone else knew I was behaving immaturely at best and sinfully at worst.

Since we can't change what we can't identify, ask God to show you any areas of your life that may be harmful to you, offensive to the people around you, or displeasing to God himself.

Talk to Me

God speaks to us in many ways. He speaks through his Word. He speaks through circumstances. He speaks through his Spirit. And he speaks through people. As you seek God, listen carefully to what he might say to you through the people around you. Proverbs 15:31 – 32 says, "He who *listens to a life-giving rebuke* will be at home among the wise. He who ignores discipline despises himself, but whoever heeds correction gains understanding" (NIV 1984 ed., emphasis mine).

I love the phrase "life-giving rebuke." Occasionally, God will send someone to communicate a strong and important message through a life-giving rebuke. It's important to note, not all rebukes are life-giving and helpful. Certainly you've been broadsided by some life-*taking* rebukes. You know, when some jerk criticizes or belittles you in a hurtful way or over something insignificant that allows the jerk to look better than you. Instead of making things better, they make things worse.

But there are times that a loving person gives a life-giving rebuke. They care about you enough to confront you lovingly. Like the church members who tried to help me see how my crude humor was hurting the church, loving people may take some risks to help you see the truth. When they do, listen.

For several years, loved ones tried to help me with another one of my blind spots. As a pastor, I prided myself in relating well with other people — showing grace, kindness, and patience. Though I was convinced I was good at interacting socially, several close people told me that I wasn't as good as I thought.

Amy was among several who expressed that I really needed to improve my people skills. She explained soberly that I often looked distracted, rushed, or bored when talking to people in the lobby after church. I replied truthfully that I often did feel distracted, rushed, or bored, but only because there were so many other people to talk to, and I had lots to do — and to top it off, some people were boring! They blab on and on and on and on. To me, if I wasn't good with people, it was someone else's fault.

After years of listening to me defend myself, Amy and a couple of her friends showed me what I do when talking to people. With a playful spirit, they acted like they were me talking to someone else. They showed me how my body language communicated disinterest, as I'd look around the room or act distracted. They demonstrated how I'd often turn slightly away from the person talking to me.

When they showed me how I acted, I defended myself, saying, "Sure, I might do that, but it's on purpose. I'm sending a subtle signal that I can't talk forever because there are many more people who need my attention." As the words came out of my mouth, I had the same feeling as when I looked at my daughter in the crowd.

Busted again.

I truly love the people that I lead. But my actions, words, and body language had been communicating the opposite. Once I listened to those closest to me, I could finally make improvements. Now I work hard to focus on the person who is in front of me, putting my whole heart into the conversation. Several people have expressed that they have noticed the change and cite tremendous improvement.

Please listen to what your loved ones have been trying to tell you. If more than one person has told you that you have a problem with something, chances are pretty good you have a problem. If all your close friends worry about you because you overspend each month, you likely have a problem with overspending. If your parents, best friends, sorority sisters, and co-workers all tell you that you are dating a good-for-nothing jerk, you are probably dating well below yourself. If everyone you love and trust expresses concern about your eating habits and weight, you probably should put the fork down and listen.

Now would be a good time to stop and ask yourself honestly, "Is there something that God has been trying to show me through his Word or trusted people that I need to hear?" I can promise you that if you'll listen, God will speak to you as you read prayerfully through this book. If you think you are without fault, remember Scripture says in 1 John 1:8, "If we claim to be without sin, we deceive ourselves and the truth is not in us." I'm praying that God will move the deception out of our hearts so the truth can come in.

Truth in Action

When God reveals spiritual toxins that need to be cleansed, I pray you will have the courage to act swiftly and decisively. James said it well in 1:22, "Do not merely listen to the word, and so deceive yourselves. Do what it says."

When we know the Word and don't do what it says, we are in direct disobedience to God — living a toxic life that he cannot bless. When God shows you what to do, do it immediately. I've heard it said that "delayed obedience is disobedience."

If you're living with your boyfriend or girlfriend and know you shouldn't be compromising, move out or get married. If the number of Twitter followers or Facebook friends has become an idol to you, it's time to tear that idol down until you can manage it in a healthy fashion. If you are consumed with worry, call it what it is: a sin. You are distrusting the promises and power of God. Quit sanctifying the sin of worry by calling it "concern" and do what it takes to renew your mind with God's truth. If you believe you are fat but you weigh only 107 pounds, admit that you have a problem. It's time to get help.

You can't change what you don't see. It's time to see the truth. You may be tempted to argue, "But I'm not a bad person." May I say respectfully and lovingly, "Yes, you are — and so am I." We are all selfish, sinful people. The Bible tells us our hearts are deceitful above all things. Jesus — the only one who is good — is the remedy for our poison.

When you clearly identify what is slowly killing you (which is far more difficult than it sounds), you can take the toxic influences to

Jesus for cleansing, purifying, and healing. When we identify the lies we so readily tell ourselves, his truth can set us free.

By God's power, we must drop the masks and tell the truth. Think about it. Why do we so readily deceive ourselves? The answer is simple and life transforming: we deceive ourselves because we are afraid of the truth. The very thing we fear is what we need most. Because when we know the truth, the truth will set us free (John 8:32).

Stop lying to yourself, swallowing the poisonous self-deceptions that keep you from experiencing healthy spiritual growth. Admit the truth. Come clean. If you're willing, the truth will set you free.

2

Septic Thoughts

Overcoming Our False Beliefs

Thought is the sculptor who can create the person you want to be.

—Henry David Thoreau

When I was in high school, I studied several years of French. I studied hard and made good grades, so of course I thought I was ready to translate for the United Nations or to work in the US Embassy in Paris. When a foreign exchange student — I'll call her Claire — moved to our school, it was my first opportunity to try my "*Bonjour, comment allez-vous*" skills out in a real conversation, not just in the classroom. The fact that she was cute and a bit cosmopolitan compared with the other girls in our school might have affected my motives as well.

Even though I had always made A's in French class, the first few minutes of my attempt at conversation with Claire didn't go far. When she spoke to me in French, I'd hear what she said in French. Then, in my mind, I'd slowly translate her French words into English. Then I would think in English. I'd craft my response in English then carefully translate it into French — all still in my mind. Once I'd taken these tedious steps, I'd attempt to reply in French and then do the whole exercise over again. Needless to say, figuring out the right French verb declensions isn't very attractive. It's hard to look cool when you're stumbling over words the way Inspector Clouseau trips over furniture in *The Pink Panther*.

After about a half-hour, though, something changed in the conversation between us. When my *nouvelle amie* Claire spoke in French, for the first time ever, I actually thought in French. Because I heard and thought in her language, I didn't have to laboriously translate back and forth between the two languages in my mind. Instead, the words started to roll off my tongue. Before long, we were talking like we'd been friends for years.

Lost in Translation

If you've ever learned to speak a foreign language, you can relate to the way this shift occurs. One of the greatest stumbling blocks to spiritual growth emerges when we get stuck in our negative, untrue, and impure thoughts instead of making the translation to God's Word. We lose momentum because we get tired of trying harder and feeling hopeless. I could easily have gotten frustrated and quit trying to communicate with the new exchange student. It felt too hard and not worth the effort.

However, by persevering, I grew in my ability to understand and speak French and also made a relational connection. I'm convinced that when left to our own native language of negativity, we lose sight of the spiritual truth that can set us free. Sadly, so many of us refuse to push through the clutter and clamor of negative thinking and false beliefs that can bombard us.

"I'm no good. I'll always fail. I'll never amount to anything."

"My life doesn't matter. No one really cares about me. If I disappeared, no one would notice, much less care."

"No matter how hard I try, I'll never make a difference. It seems like I mess up everything I do."

"God could never love me. After all I've done, why would God care about me? I'm worthless."

"My life stinks. And it's only going to get worse. I'll never get a break. There's no way I can change the way I am."

"I have to take care of myself. No one else, especially God, comes through for me. I better grab whatever I can whenever I get the chance."

Any one of these thoughts can be deadly, and cumulatively they can imprison us in a hellish well of toxic waste. If we want to break free into the exhilarating freedom of God's truth, then we must begin by accurately diagnosing our problem. As we discussed in the last chapter, you can't overcome a sin that you can't identify.

The root of most sins we commit outwardly is the false beliefs we embrace inwardly. In order to experience a life of purity with a clean heart, we must identify and reject the toxic thoughts that keep us from God's best. We don't need Dr. Phil to tell us what God revealed to us in his Word thousands of years ago: your thoughts determine who you become. Proverbs 23:7 says, "For as [a person] thinks in his heart, so is he" (NKJV).

If you think negative and toxic thoughts, you'll become a negative and sick person. Your soul will stagnate and wither. If you think God's truth in your thoughts, you'll become like Christ. Your soul will flow with living water and flourish. If you're not trying to translate the negative into positive truth, if you're not willing to focus on God's absolutes instead of your own mental chatter, then you'll only drift farther away from what you desire most.

Most of life's battles are won or lost in the mind. Abraham Lincoln said, "I want to know all God's thoughts. All the rest are just details." Our thoughts are either focused on what's eternal, life-changing, and true, or lost in the details of our temporary, selfish, false beliefs. If you're a Christian, then you're fully aware of the battle between your flesh (your earthly desires) and your spirit (your heavenly desires).

This ongoing battle between flesh and spirit is usually fought in our minds. For example, a husband doesn't wake up one morning and decide he's going to cheat on his wife that day. Instead it's a gradual process of sliding away thought by thought that allows him to begin an adulterous relationship. If we want to win the physical battle, we have to control the spiritual battlefield. And Scripture makes it clear how we can control the battlefield: "Carefully guard your thoughts because they are the source of true life" (Prov. 4:23 CEV).

Mind Games

Like a firewall protecting your computer, you need to remain vigilant against Satan's lies that threaten to corrupt the hard drive of your mind. We have to know what we're fighting against, what we're fighting for, and how to spot the enemy. Paul makes our strategy clear and concise in his teaching to the Corinthians: "The weapons we fight with are not the weapons of the world. On the contrary, they have divine power to demolish strongholds" (2 Cor. 10:4).

The Greek root word translated as "strongholds" here is *ochuroma*. As a noun it can be translated as "castle," or as a verb, "to fortify." A literal translation for Paul's usage would be a "prisoner locked by deception." As Christians, we have stronger weapons than knives, guns, and grenades. We have faith, prayer, and God's Word. God wants us to use his weapons to win the battle of the mind. God's truth releases us from the prison of lies.

Unfortunately, many believers are held hostage by toxic lies. We hold the key in our minds but lose sight of it in the junk drawer of our negative thoughts. This explains Paul's message as he continues in his letter to the church at Corinth: "We demolish arguments and every pretension that sets itself up against the knowledge of God, and we take captive every thought to make it obedient to Christ" (2 Cor. 10:5). Any thought that is not from God should be demolished, destroyed, annihilated. Instead of being prisoners of war, we take untrue thoughts captive and make them obedient to God's truth. We can win the mind games.

How? From my study of God's Word, my own experiences, as well as the shared experiences of others, I've identified four specific kinds of toxic waste that can poison our minds: (1) *pessimism*, which usually produces chronically negative thoughts; (2) *anxiety*, which usually manifests as fearful and worried thoughts; (3) *bitterness*, which pollutes our thinking with discontented and envious thoughts; and (4) *criticism*, which pumps destructive judgmental thoughts into our minds. To help you identify your own areas of thought-bondage, let's look at each one and how it can be overcome.

Weed Salad

Take a minute to survey your thought life. Do you battle with chronically negative thoughts about yourself, others, or life in general? Maybe in your self-talk, you tell yourself, "I don't have what it takes. No matter how hard I try, I'll never get ahead. No matter what I do, I always get the short end of the stick. My life is always going to stink."

Or perhaps you are often overwhelmed with too much to do. No matter how hard you work, there's always more. You slave away with little or no hope for relief. While you might actually have a lot on your plate, your negative thoughts only compound the problem. "I just can't do it all. There's just way too much. No one appreciates me anyway. All I do is give, give, give. Everyone else drains me dry. I don't know how much longer I can take it."

It could be that your negative thought patterns tend to surface in more mundane areas of life. You might find yourself complaining, "My hair looks awful — it never does what I want it to do." "I've got nothing to wear and can't afford to buy anything I'd enjoy wearing anyway." "We're out of food again? Do the kids think we're made of money?" "I can't believe I wasted my money on this stupid book!" (I hope you're not thinking this last thought, but you never know.)

Even if a grain of truth exists in a particular thought, where you plant the seed determines how — and if — it will grow. If you let weeds grow in your garden too long, they will choke out the truth and smother your joy. You'll be forced to eat weed salad because they've overtaken the good fruit you wanted to grow there.

Weed the garden of your mind on a regular basis. What needs pruning? What needs to be nipped in the bud before it overtakes the fruit of the Spirit your soul longs to produce?

High Anxiety

A close cousin to negative thinking is fearful thinking. You may be able to quote the verse that says, "God has not given us a spirit of fear," even while your thought life is haunted by a host of fearful spirits. Like a lot of people, you might be consumed with economic fears. "What's going to happen to the economy? Do you think I could lose more of my 401k? What if my taxes go up again? What if my company downsizes and I get laid off?"

Or you might be overwhelmed with relational fears. You love your spouse, but he or she continues to disappoint you. Marriage isn't what you hoped it would be. "Will we be able to work things out? Or do I just settle for less and keep quiet? Does he still love me?" "Will she ever pay as much attention to me again as she used to?" Maybe you hope to get married but aren't sure if you can really trust anyone. "What if I never get married? My clock is ticking by the second. How can you ever really trust someone anyway? Most people I've met are looking out only for themselves. I'm probably destined to stay single for the rest of my life."

If you're a parent, chances are good that you often worry about your kids. You know you shouldn't worry, but it's hard not to get anxious when you consider the world today. "What if my children get mixed up with the wrong crowd? I hope they aren't drinking, having sex, or doing drugs. There are so many bad influences. I can't sleep at night thinking about all the dangers facing my children."

I struggle with this particular toxic thought category as much as anyone. Even when I know it's irrational, I still find myself riding a bullet train of worry all the way to the last stop at High Anxiety. If Amy is running late coming home, my mind starts to wander. Has she been in an accident? If so, she could be dead. I can't live without her. Wait, if she's dead, I've got to get her funeral ready. I'm the pastor, but there's no way I could do my wife's funeral. Then what's going to happen to me? How can I ever help the kids get over this? And how will my life go on? No one would ever marry a guy with six kids.

Okay, so now you know how you can pray for me. We all have our problems, don't we?

Dissatisfaction Guaranteed

Although most people alive today are more blessed than anyone in the history of the world, it is still so easy to be consumed with discontent. Amid the bounty of blessings we experience daily, thoughts of dissatisfaction pop up like pimples on a teenager. Maybe you battle with discounted thoughts about your body or appearance. "I don't like my body. I wish I looked different. No matter what I do, I just don't measure up physically."

Or maybe you are locked in on dating someone. You don't feel complete or whole without someone of the opposite sex by your side. "I can't be happy unless I'm dating someone. And all the good ones seem to be taken. I guess this one will do for now but not forever. Can anyone really love me anyway?"

If you have those thoughts while you're unmarried, chances are good you'll find more reasons to be dissatisfied once you tie the knot. "I wish my husband were a better provider ... or spiritual leader ... or communicator ... or lover ... or whatever." "I wish my wife didn't nag all the time, telling me she wishes I were a better provider ... or spiritual leader ... or communicator ... or lover ... or whatever."

And the list goes on. "I wish we had children ... or more children ... or different children. I wish they were smarter or more attractive or better athletes." Don't forget material dissatisfaction. "I wish we had a better car ... or more money ... or nicer clothes ... or better vacations ... or a bigger house with a bigger kitchen with granite countertops and a third car garage for the boat that I wish I had but can't afford because I work at this stupid job that I don't like for way less money than I'm really worth."

Critical Mass

Perhaps without even knowing it, you are consumed with criticizing anything that crosses your path. You can find fault with people, buildings, companies, churches, today's lunch menu, or anything else you encounter. You meet someone and instantly think, "I can't believe she's dressed like that — surely, she knows how trashy she looks in that dress. And way too much makeup. Just listen to her name-dropping — give me a break." Or maybe you look at someone and think critical thoughts: "I'd never do that. Who does he think he is? He's so full of himself — what a jerk."

At work, you might find your thoughts constantly drifting toward criticism. "This place is a zoo and so beneath where I should be working. The people I work with are a bunch of idiots. The whole place would fall apart without me. Why do I stay here anyway?"

Or you walk into a church for the first time (something you find yourself doing a lot since you go to the same church only until you find something you can't stand about it). "This building looks like a strip mall — oh, it actually used to be one. These people aren't friendly at all. The music is too loud, too rock 'n' roll [or traditional or old-fashioned or progressive]. The pastor is so boring. The coffee is so weak — definitely not dark roast and I'm sure it's not Fair Trade. Even their donuts are stale."

Pause for a moment. Think about your thoughts. Be brutally

honest. Do you battle with negative thoughts about yourself, other people, or life in general? Are you often consumed with fearful, worrisome thoughts, putting your faith in bad things happening rather than good? Do you find yourself discontented, always wishing life were different or better? Are you occasionally or often critical, finding something wrong with a lot of people, places, or things? If you answered yes to one or more of the previous questions, your life is being infected by toxic thoughts. You are losing the battle of the mind. It's time to fight to win.

After you take a good hard look, jump in and grab those nasty thoughts and the chain of self-talk they usually bring with them. If there's anything you think that God would find unholy and displeasing, flag it. Negative, fearful, discontented, critical thoughts are not allowed or tolerated. They are your prisoners. You are not theirs.

Thought Taste Test

Once you have identified toxic thoughts, it's time to take action and replace the lies with truth. In Philippians, Paul said, "The peace of God, which transcends all understanding, will guard your hearts and your minds in Christ Jesus" (4:7). As you meditate on God, he will protect your mind. Furthermore, you will be filled with what you feast upon in your mind. As Paul explained it, "Finally, brothers and sisters, whatever is true ... noble ... right ... pure ... lovely ... admirable — if anything is excellent or praiseworthy — think about such things" (Phil. 4:8). When you think God thoughts, he will guard your mind with peace. Instead of meditating on poison, you will meditate on truth. You might not see an overnight change in your life, but if you direct your thoughts toward God, I promise you that over time your life will be more joyful and peace-filled than you can imagine.

Once you acquire a taste for wholesome thoughts and godly thinking, your mental palate becomes more sensitive to the taste of poison. I was reminded of this benefit recently when my wife and I were forced to discern the truth about a situation with some good friends of ours. Amy and I have been friends with a particular couple for many years. We've shared countless dinners together, watched dozens of plays, performances, and sporting events of each other's children, and exchanged Christmas presents for more than two decades.

All the more reason that we were so devastated when a woman told me our friends were talking badly about our family.

We were crushed and felt so betrayed. How could our close friends say such things? We thought about calling them and letting them have it. We started making new plans for Friday night to avoid seeing our friends at a church event. We contemplated taking our kids out of the activities our kids shared with theirs.

As our thoughts raced straight into the ditch, Amy finally put the brakes on and said, "Hold on a second. Who told you our friends said that bad stuff about our family?" When I told Amy the name of the lady, she quickly reminded me that we didn't know her well. And we did know our friends extremely well. For years, our friends had always been loyal, faithful, and full of integrity.

That's when Amy and I agreed to grab our thoughts and take them captive. Instead of allowing our thoughts to fill with poison based on a rumor, we'd *choose* to believe the best about our friends.

Our thoughts are ours. And we'd make the better choice. So we decided to channel our minds in a direction that would honor God.

We didn't call our friends and let them have it. We didn't remove our kids from their common events with friends. And we did go to the church event and see our friends, who were as wonderful as they had ever been.

Several weeks later, the lady who had told me the disheartening news apologized and explained that she had made a mistake. We were so thankful that we didn't let our thoughts take us somewhere we never should have gone. We were so grateful for being able to taste our thoughts and recognize the bitter bite of poison.

The Road-Kill Diet

This experience provides us with a great picture of the choices we have when we confront our thoughts. When we hear something that is not true, we first have to discern the lie. We might slow down to ask ourselves, Is this true? To answer, we might have to think, What does the Bible say about this? Once we determine that the thought is not from God, we have to determine what is from God. Then we choose to think the godlike thoughts instead. For a while, it might be a step-by-step process, sort of like when I was trying to converse in French and had to stop and translate each idea word for word.

After a while, though, our minds will be made new, different, and filled with truth. We'll become fluent in God's truth and be able to exterminate the false ideas trying to feed on our faith. Instinctively we'll recognize poisonous thoughts and reject them before they stain our thoughts. Instead we'll think things that are true, noble, right, pure, lovely, and admirable. If anything is excellent or praiseworthy, we will think about those things. Without hesitation, we'll reject thoughts that are not from God. And naturally (or supernaturally), we'll think God's kind of thoughts.

You will always find what you are looking for. Think about the difference between two birds: a vulture and a hummingbird. Vultures soar high in the sky, looking and searching. What does a vulture find? Dead things. The ugly oversized bird doesn't stop until he finds lifeless, rotting road kill. Contrast the vulture to the tiny hummingbird. With wings flapping twenty beats a second, what does this small bird find? Not dead things and disgusting rancid meat, but instead, sweet, life-giving nectar. Daily, each bird finds what he is looking for.

The same is true for you. You can be on a road-kill diet or you can find nectar in each day. It's up to you, because you will find what you search for. If you want to find things to be negative about or to worry about, it is not hard to do. If you plan to be critical, you don't have to look far to find fault. If you choose to be negative, you'll easily accomplish your goal. But if you want to see the good in life, you can find it everywhere. If you choose to watch for places God is working, you'll see his loving presence each place you look. If you decide to look for hope, faith, and a better future, you will discover these positive things and more countless times a day.

Decide the destination of your mind. Any time your mind drifts toward dangerous thoughts, stop. Grab those runaway thoughts. Do whatever it takes to get the trash out of your mind. An Old Testament prophet said to God, "You see me and test my *thoughts* about you.

Drag them off like sheep to be butchered! Set them apart for the day of slaughter!" (Jer. 12:3, emphasis mine). Can you hear the passion for truth in Jeremiah's words? He asked God to test his thoughts, identify any that were "black sheep," drag them off, and butcher them.

Are you willing to ask God to do the same with your thought life?

Mind Makeover: God Edition

Maybe you're thinking, "Okay, Craig, I appreciate your little pep talk on positive thinking and how God wants us to see the glass is half full, not half empty." Please don't limit what I'm saying to self-affirmations and positive thinking. I'm not saying you shape your life with good thoughts. I'm saying you shape it with God thoughts.

Remove anything that is not from God. Align your thoughts with his Word. If your life is continually corrupted with unhealthy thoughts, wash them with the water of the Word (see Eph. 5:26). Just as white water rapids soften the jagged edges of rocks into smooth river stones, so does God's truth transform the shards of our broken thoughts into a firm foundation upon which we can build our faith.

You are not a victim of your thoughts. You have the power through Christ to take them captive. As a result, you will find what you are looking for. You can believe the worst or think the best. You can find reasons to worry or reasons to have faith. You can live pessimistically, or you can possess life-changing faith.

The world is full of spiritual toxins, but your mind will not be overcome. Paul reminds us of the supernatural antidote to the poisons that try to infect our minds in Romans 12:2: "Do not conform to the pattern of this world, but be transformed by the *renewing of your mind*" (emphasis mine). The Greek word translated as "renewing" is *anakainosis*, which means "to restore, to renovate, to make better than new." I envision an old, termite-infested house being transformed by a good exterminator and a construction crew from HGTV. Think of it as "Mind Makeover: God Edition"!

If you want to live a clean life in a polluted world, you must remove the seeds of poison from within. Practice taking every thought captive. Ask God to identify and help remove the life-draining ideas and images from your mind. Fill your thoughts with his truth and the beauty of his goodness. Renew your mind and watch your faith grow in ways that will astound you.

3

Lethal Language

Experiencing the Power of Life-Giving Words

Words which do not give the light of Christ increase the darkness.
—Mother Teresa

It was a cool, late October afternoon when I finally learned the truth. Until then, I'd lived my first ten years in blissful ignorance, sheltered from the painful revelation that was about to shatter my world. Ashley Sanders, my fifth-grade neighbor and playmate, swung next to me on her backyard swing set. As she pumped her legs forward toward the sky, her golden hair caught in the breeze. Peaking at the top of her swinging arc, she gracefully tucked her legs under the wooden swing seat as gravity pulled her backward.

Not to be outdone, I leaned back and shot my legs straight out so that I might swing slightly higher than Ashley, intent on impressing her with my skillful swinging ability. For a brief few minutes, life couldn't have been better — the wind on my face, the cutest girl in class by my side, the sun in her hair. Then Ashley blindsided me with a life-changing bombshell.

"You have an ugly profile," she said very matter-of-factly, in the same way that she might say, "It's really hot today," or "We're having Hamburger Helper for dinner."

Did I hear her right? Ugly? Me? No way!

My fifth-grade dream girl then added an "I'm way better looking than you and wouldn't want you for my boyfriend if you were the only guy in town" look.

My body went numb from the shock and awe of her attack. Stunned, I hung on for dear life, no longer concerned with swinging higher, but afraid I'd fall off.

"I do not!" I shouted back. Even though I didn't know what a profile is, the word *ugly* associated with anything about my manly fifth-grade form immediately put me on the defensive.

"You do too," Ashley said flatly, her voice void of any human emotion. Then she fired at me again, punching each word for impact in that sing-song point-blank range mastered only by a princess of the playground: "You have an ugly profile."

My mind raced. What is a profile? A garden tool? A kitchen gadget? A professional filer? Are there amateur filers?

Fearing I might compromise my ironclad "I do not" defense, I nonetheless swallowed hard and asked, "So, uh, what's a profile, anyway?"

"Stupid," she fired back. "It's how you look from the side." Looking at me from the side as she continued to swing, she dropped the final painful truth on me. "You have an ugly profile because your nose is soooo big."

Time stood still.

Big nose? Me? What was she talking about? My nose is a normal nose. There's nothing special or out of the ordinary about my regular, everyday, perfectly average-sized nose.

I abandoned my battle post and ran home as fast as I could. Could it be true? Do I have a big nose? Blowing past my little sister, I dashed into the bathroom to see for myself. Praying for the best and bracing for the worst, I grabbed my mom's hand mirror and perched on the counter by the sink. I turned my head to the side and tilted the hand mirror to an angle reflecting into the larger bathroom mirror. At that moment, it dawned on me. I'd seen myself in mirrors only from the front view for my entire life. From the front, my nose looked normal. But from the side ...

It was true — I had considerably more nose than the average guy. "Ahhhhhhhhhhh!" I shouted, shocked by what I saw. Ashley Sanders, though somewhat cruel, didn't lie. I did have a big nose. Big noses make ugly profiles.

My life would never be the same.

Sticks and Stones

You don't have to have a big nose to have heard the childhood mantra, "Sticks and stones may break my bones, but words can never hurt me." Just because it's spouted by first graders doesn't mean it's true. The Ashley Sanders incident remains a classic case in point for me. Perhaps the adult translation of this age-old adage is more like, "Sticks and stones can bruise your body for a few days, but words can scar your soul for life."

Like a neutron bomb which annihilates human life but leaves buildings intact, words can devastate. Your body may remain unharmed, but your heart suffers the deadly shrapnel of painful phrases. David, who knew a thing or two about having enemies in high places, wrote that evildoers "sharpen their tongues like swords and aim cruel words like deadly arrows" (Ps. 64:3). Whether you're eighteen or eighty, you can probably recall the pain of someone's harsh words scalding your soul. Maybe you still hear the message from years ago, playing an endless loop in your mind, echoing inside you every day:

"You'll never amount to anything."
"I wish I never had you."
"You're nothing like your brother."
"I'm sick of you."
"I never loved you."
"You'll never change."

As devastating as these words can be, they can be offset by words of truth, hope, and love. The right words at the right time can be helpful, healing, and life-transforming. Proverbs 18:21 says, "The tongue has the power of life and death." What you say can give life to you and to other people, or it can take life away.

Words are powerful beyond imagination. Think about it. When

God created the world, how did he do it? He spoke. God said, "Let there be ..." and there was. Words have power. In so many fairy tales, legends, and myths, it's the power of a spoken spell, incantation, or magic phrase that can either cause destruction or restore harmony.

The potency of godly words can revive, heal, and change our lives. Ungodly words have the power to bind, imprison, and destroy.

Creative words create.

Destructive words destroy.

Hurtful words crush.

Helpful words build up.

Toxic words poison.

Soothing words heal.

Faith-filled words bring life.

Faithless words bring death.

Countless times a day, when it comes to what you hear and say, you have choices to make. When you hear the words of others, you can choose to receive them as truth or reject them as lies. And every time you open your mouth to utter a word, you have the opportunity to speak life or the temptation to take it. Think back through the past few days. When you spoke to others, what did they hear? Either you aimed sharp, poison-tipped darts at their hearts, or you injected them with life-giving, God-honoring booster shots.

Both Sides of Your Mouth

Several passages in the Bible clearly contrast the difference. Proverbs says, "The words of the reckless pierce like swords, but the tongue of the wise brings healing" (12:18). What are reckless words? They're the shards of glass you hurl in the heat of an argument. They're the words you know you'll regret as soon as they've left your tongue. They're the bitter, painful, cancerous messages that leave people sick and hurting. Talking out of the other side of your mouth, the tongue of the wise brings encouragement, joy, and wisdom. Proverbs 15:4 expresses this duality another way: "The soothing tongue is a tree of life, but a perverse tongue crushes the spirit." Positive words plant seeds for beautiful trees. Deceptive words poison others like weed killer.

What are the phrases etched in your memory that have shaped your life? If you are like most people, you can recall several of the many toxic phrases that have been directed at you. They could have been innocent: "Did you mean to do that to your hair?" "Why aren't you married yet?" "I thought you would do much better than that."

Or perhaps the words were intended to pierce your heart like a poison dagger: "Why can't you do anything right?" "I wish I'd never married you." "You're a real piece of work." "You are the biggest disappointment to me."

My hope is that you can also remember life-giving words spoken to you at the precise moment you needed them. Maybe someone told you, "I believe in you," and it was all you needed to move forward. It could've been someone saying, "I'm so proud of you," and their affirmation touched your soul. Maybe a close friend shared, "I'm more thankful for you than you could ever know," and in return, those words meant more to you than your friend would ever know. The words spoken by a loving spouse can often communicate, "I'd marry you all over again," reminding you of their support.

Another proverb compares such words to honey and to medicine: "Gracious words are a honeycomb, sweet to the soul and healing to the bones" (Prov. 16:24). I'm thankful for the people in my life who fed me sweet words of affirmation and encouragement.

Amy's words have often kept me going. When I'm down and feeling inadequate for the ministry before me, she reminds me who I am and what I have in Christ. When others criticize our style of ministry, she reminds me that God called us to do a different work. And sometimes, she simply calls me her Mega-man! I may be an average guy, but I like knowing that I'm her superhero.

God has used both my mom and dad to build me up with strong affirmation. For as long as I can remember, Mom repeatedly told me, "You can do anything you set your mind to. God has given you tremendous gifts, and I know he has amazing plans for your life." Each time she spoke those words, she planted seeds of faith in my heart that years later grew and bloomed into the ministry we have today.

My dad had his own way of investing in me with his words. When I played baseball as a kid, after I made a great play or hit a home run, Dad always beamed and said, "Son, I'm so proud of you the buttons burst off my shirt." For years I had no idea what he meant, but I sure knew I liked it.

Now that I'm older, my parents' affirmation still means more to me than I can express. My dad sent me a card once to congratulate me on what God has done through our ministry. In keeping with his baseball passion, he simply wrote, "You are in the major leagues now, son. I couldn't be more proud of you." I still tear up each time I read his words.

Take Out the Trash

We obviously can't control what others say about us, but we can control what we believe. Since toxic words can destroy our souls, we've got to passionately guard our hearts against them. Do whatever it takes to keep the poison out of your heart. Solomon told his son, "Listen closely to *my words* ... Above all else, guard your heart, for it is the wellspring of life" (Prov. 4:20, 23, NIV 1984 ed., emphasis mine). With his life-giving words, a protective father warned his son to guard his heart as his life source. We must keep others from dumping their toxic waste into our water supply.

God helped me do this during a pivotal time in my early years of ministry. Between the ages of twenty-three and twenty-eight, I served as an associate pastor at First United Methodist Church, a thriving downtown church in Oklahoma City. My pastor, Nick Harris, was extraordinarily gifted and a great mentor to me. Though very effective, his style of leadership and philosophy of church proved somewhat controversial within this traditional denomination. Some United Methodist conference leaders embraced Pastor Nick's philosophies as necessary and effective. Other conference leaders felt he pushed the limits too far. Because I was one of "Nick's boys," I probably came under a little extra scrutiny during the ordination process.

At the time, the Methodist Church recognized me as what they called a "local pastor." Though I was not ordained, they blessed me to marry, bury, baptize, and serve communion under Pastor Nick's leadership. Midway through seminary, at the age of twenty-six, I sat before the ordaining board. The leader of the board happened to be a guy who didn't like Nick's style and philosophy and apparently didn't think highly of me.

Looking back, I acknowledge that I had some rough edges that needed to be knocked off. Even knowing the leader of the ordaining crew wasn't one of my biggest fans, I was still stunned when he delivered their verdict. "Craig," the leader said soberly, "you don't have the normal gift-set that most pastors have. After lots of discussion, we're not sure you are called to full-time ministry."

His two sentences turned my life upside down.

I felt like I'd been punched in the stomach and couldn't breathe. My mind raced. What's going to happen? What will everyone think? Did I miss God's calling? Can I face my church, my wife, my friends? A few words from this committee were about to redirect everything I believed was right, true, and pleasing to God.

As I drove home from the meeting in my little Geo Prism, tears flooded down my cheeks. I pulled the car over and cried out to God, "What is happening? I was certain you called me to serve you in ministry!"

I'm not one to throw out the God-spoke-to-me card loosely. Without question, I know God speaks to people, but I'm very careful not to say, "God told me . . ." casually. But at that moment, I truly believe God spoke to me. It wasn't audible, but it was crystal clear. I was pierced by the committee leader's words, and God ministered to me with soothing balm: "You are not who others say you are. You are who I say you are, and I say you are called to serve me in ministry."

God's message gave me the strength I needed to drive to the church and talk to my pastor. After breaking the news to him, I saw

Nick look at me compassionately and smile a knowing smile. He explained that the ordaining board said the same thing to him years ago. Then Nick sealed my faith when he spoke words that would carry me for years to come: "When God calls you, there's not a person in the world that can stop you from doing what God wants you to do."

That was all I needed.

I may be rejected by men (and Ashley Sanders), but I'm approved by God.

I certainly wasn't the first to experience such a wound, and I won't be the last. But I made a choice: to reject the toxic words of men and embrace God's affirmation by his Spirit and through my pastor. Words of truth kept me going. I am doing what I'm doing today because words of life empowered me to move forward. (For the record, the board approved me a year later to be ordained as a deacon, one step below full ordination as an elder. After leaving the denomination, I still have great appreciation for their tradition and ministry.)

When someone says something to or about you, train yourself to categorize the words the same way we train our kids with a game our friends taught us, Truth or Trash. Analyze the message and source before swallowing and digesting what someone else wants to feed you. Are their words true? Based in Scripture? Supported by data over time? If so, embrace them. Allow those life-giving words to minister to your soul and conform you to the image of Christ. If their words are untrue, mean-spirited, and critical without being constructive, then call them what they are — toxic waste. Reject those words. Don't let them into your soul. Take out the trash and leave it by the curb. Delete toxic words and insert the truth.

Choose Life

Not only should we hold in any words that are negative, but we should release words that are positive. I try to live by the rule, "If you think something good, say it." Every time you think something positive, give it life with your words. This is especially important if you are married.

I'm convinced this is one reason Amy and I have a strong marriage. Whenever I think something about her that might bless her, I try to say it immediately. (And that means I'm talking to her a lot!)

Recently we had a college senior stay with us for the summer. Amy and I agreed that we'd simply be ourselves instead of putting on a show. So when I saw Amy in an outfit that looked great to me, I colorfully told her how much I liked it and the next thing you know, we were lip locked. My daughter, Anna, rolled her eyes and looked at our guest and said with great enthusiasm, "Believe me when I tell you, once you've lived with them for thirty seconds, you'll get used to that. It happens all the time." We laughed and laughed about Anna's commentary on our marriage. Yet secretly I'm thankful that my daughter knows her mom and dad encourage each other affectionately.

The moment you think something good, bless someone you love with your positive words. With the use of technology, you can share life-giving words all day long. You can make a quick call just to say, "I was thinking about you." You can send an email saying you miss someone. You can send an IM calling your girlfriend your secret pet name. Or you can text a steamy message to your husband. (Amy likes to say we have great text! Just make sure you delete them so you will never be embarrassed. And be careful that you don't send them to the wrong person by mistake. Just saying.) Each time you think something good, speak it. Never rob someone of the blessings of an unspoken treasure.

Build one another up with your words. You can never offer too much encouragement. I tell Mandy, my second daughter, that I'm crazy about her. Over and over again I express my love for her. Finally one day, Mandy said, "Dad, you're always telling me how crazy you are about me. Every day it's the same thing." Fearing I might've been too repetitive, I asked her, "So do you want me to stop?" She darted back passionately, "No way, Daddy. I love it when you tell me."

If you show me a struggling relationship, I'll show you one filled with toxic words. If you show me any marriage that is limping along, I'll show you a marriage filled with word darts flying recklessly through the air. Your words matter. They are either giving life or taking life. Choose to give life.

Station Identification

As you work on speaking faith-filled and encouraging words to others, don't forget about yourself. *Self-talk* is the term used to describe the words you say to yourself or about yourself that others rarely hear. Local TV and radio stations used to break in at intervals to remind their audiences that they were part of the same community, not just some big network or nationally syndicated show. The broadcasters wanted you to remember their call letters, their identity. We must often remember our own call letters, who we really are, and not succumb to the false messages that bombard us daily.

I'm convinced that many people are limiting their futures with toxic self-talk. For example, you might find yourself thinking things like this: "I'm so exhausted. I don't think I can survive this week. My job is killing me. I'm not that good anyway. I'll probably just screw things up." In some ways, negative self-talk can become a self-fulfilling prophecy. Just as an athlete is more likely to make the shot after visualizing making it, she's also more likely to miss it after visualizing a miss. Your words, whether externally spoken or internally absorbed, shape your future.

I encourage you to constantly speak life-giving words to yourself and to your circumstances. Jesus said, "If anyone says to this mountain, 'Go, throw yourself into the sea,' and does not doubt in their heart but believes that what they say will happen, it will be done for them" (Mark 11:23). Notice how Jesus emphasizes the power of what we say, in this case, to a mountain. One pastor I know used to always say, "Don't talk about your mountain. Talk to it."

When David was just a teenaged shepherd boy, he used his words to build his faith while facing the unbeatable giant, Goliath. Listen to the words of faith David said to himself and to the giant. "David said to the Philistine, 'You come against me with sword and spear and javelin, but I come against you in the name of the LORD Almighty, the God of the armies of Israel, whom you have defied. This day the LORD will hand you over to me, and I'll strike you down and cut off your head'" (1 Sam. 17:45 – 46). If you are facing a giant in your life, speak to it. Tell your opposition, "You are not bigger than my God. With God's help I will defeat you."

To be clear, I'm not teaching what is known in church circles as "word-faith" doctrine. Some believe that you will have whatever you say. In my opinion, this is a false and dangerous belief. I'm not saying that our words have more power than God's plan. Beyond a shadow of a doubt, God is a sovereign, all-knowing, all-powerful, ever-present God. He does whatever he wants to do. Simply agree with what God says. Just as we align our thoughts with his thoughts, so should we align our words with his truth.

A Hundred Reasons to Live

Years ago I met with a guy from our church I'll call Scott. Several minutes into our conversation I could tell that he battled with a deep and dangerous depression. Trying to discern the severity of his depression, I gently asked if he ever thought about taking his own life. I wasn't surprised when he said that he thought about it all the time.

For the next twenty minutes or so, Scott told me all the reasons that he had nothing to live for. Toxic self-talk flowed like sewage through a busted dam. "I'm not good at anything. No one loves me. I'll never get married. I'm a total failure." On and on he lamented.

As a young pastor, I wasn't sure what to do, so I prayed quickly in my mind asking God for wisdom and direction. I believe God prompted me to do something that I've never done before or since. I grabbed a notepad and told Scott, "You're going to give me a hundred reasons you have to live."

He stared blankly at me as I wrote numbers, quickly making a hundred slots ready for Scott's one hundred reasons to live. So I asked him, "What's the first reason?"

Scott reiterated his hopeless stance to me, "I told you, I don't have any reasons to live."

Not backing down, I pressed him. "Tell me something that you are good at. Anything. Just tell me one thing."

Scott conceded and said emotionlessly, "Okay. I'm a pretty good writer." And he was. Scott wrote newsletters for his company and unquestionably had writing talent. "There you go," I said as confidently as I could, "Number one: you are a good writer."

"Give me number two," I continued.

Scott hesitated again. "I told you," he started as I interrupted him. "Number two?" I asked, not taking no for an answer.

"I'm funny," Scott said without cracking a smile. "People tell me I'm funny." And he was a funny guy, with a seriously dry and witty sense of humor. So I wrote down and said aloud for effect, "Number two. You are a funny guy. Number three?" I asked, not letting up.

"I look a lot like Robert Redford," Scott said, looking as serious as he could be.

Now, I don't want to undermine everything I've written in this chapter by saying something negative, but Robert Redford he was not! So I simply wrote down, while reading it slowly, "You ... are ... *very* ... funny."

He finally showed a hint of a smile. A small breakthrough.

"Number four," I said, trying to keep the ball rolling.

Before long, Scott started getting into the exercise. Evidently he did have many reasons to live that he was oblivious to moments earlier. Within a few minutes, I was filling in blanks as fast as I could write. Once Scott worked past his negative self-talk, he actually did see lots of positive traits about himself. He had a sister who looked up to him. He had a small group of people he prayed for daily. He served Thanksgiving dinner each year to the homeless. He sponsored a Compassion International child in Chile. One by one, we plowed through 100 specific and different reasons why Scott should live.

At the end of our time together, Scott seemed genuinely touched. I recommended a trained counselor that he agreed to see. Then I prayed for Scott and gave him his list of reasons to live. Several months later, Scott moved to another town and I lost track of him.

You can only imagine how shocked I was a dozen years or so later to see him walk up to me after church to introduce his wife and son. He tried to thank me for our time together but couldn't get his words out because of his tears. I'll never forget the moment when Scott reached into his pocket, pulled out his wallet, and presented to me a tattered sheet of paper with a hundred reasons why he should live. He'd carried it with him all these years as a reminder. He handed me the sheet and said, "I don't need this anymore. God has written hundreds of more reasons on my heart."

Speak to Your Mountain

When you are tempted to say, "I have way too much to do," stop and replace it with truth. "I am equipped and gifted by God, readily prepared to do everything God wants me to do." When you feel like you are just average or worse, call that what it is: trash. Tell yourself, "I am the workmanship of God, created in Christ Jesus to do good works which God prepared in advance for me to do." If you feel too bad for God to use, remind yourself of the truth.

"I am a new creation in Christ.

"The old has gone.

"The new has come."

When you feel like you are going to always be miserable, speak to that mountain. "I have everything I need. God is my source of joy and life." When you feel like you are facing a giant too big to overcome, look up to him and say, "I have all the faith I need for this. Who are you to come against my God? Today my God will give me the victory."

You have the power to create life through your words. You also have the ability to take life using the power of lethal language. You have the power to slay giants and the power to lay down in front of them. You have the power to move mountains and the power to curse them for being in your way. The choice is yours.

It's all a matter of what you say and how you say it.

4

Hazardous Waste

Uncovering Our Hidden Sins

Sin is not hurtful because it is forbidden, but it is forbidden because it is hurtful.

—Benjamin Franklin

Have you ever been caught in a lie? If you said no, I'm guessing you were just caught again! I'm just as guilty as anyone. In fact, I recently took the meaning of *busted* to a whole new level. Since Amy and I have six kids, many people inevitably think we're a little crazy. To them, deliberately having that many children is inconceivable (pun apology extended).

So when they say things like, "Six kids! Don't you know what causes that?" I love to have a little fun. I say, "As a matter of fact, we *do* know what causes it, and we're not willing to give it up!" Amy has heard my shtick so many times now that she usually walks away. She knows that I often go on to complain that she can't keep her hands off me since she thinks about only one thing. People roll their eyes (and probably say a prayer for my poor wife), but it doesn't stop me from having fun.

Joking about our "basketball team with a sub" is one of my favorite icebreakers when I'm speaking in a new venue. Before a big leaders' conference this year in Atlanta, Amy made me promise that I wouldn't tell my she-won't-keep-her-hands-off-me jokes. Reluctantly, I agreed and fully *intended* to keep my word. Ten minutes or so into my talk, however, I off-handedly mentioned having six kids. Before I knew it, I did the whole routine, including the line, "I beg my wife just to cuddle, but she keeps pushing me until I give in." Honestly, it was pretty funny. But breaking my promise to Amy wasn't.

To make matters worse, when I talked to her on the phone afterward, she asked if I made any jokes about our marriage. I'm not proud of what I'm about to tell you, and that's the truth. I decided to gamble and lie to my wife after already breaking my promise to her. "No, I don't think I mentioned anything about you, sweetheart," I said, holding my breath and praying she wouldn't find out. Then she asked, "Then why did I see all those tweets from people at the conference talking about how I want you all the time?"

Like I said, *really* busted.

Sticky Situation

My failure with Amy wasn't the first, and I fear it won't be the last. Unfortunately, because of our fallen nature, everyone eventually gives in to temptation and chooses their own way over God's way. Usually, our sin snowballs into an avalanche of deception. Like Adam and Eve in the garden, our first response to sinning is usually covering it up. When the first people on earth disobeyed God's one rule — to avoid the fruit from the Tree of Knowledge of Good and Evil — they didn't immediately run to God and apologize. Instead they did the same thing I did when Amy asked me her question. They lied and tried to cover up their disobedience.

True to our fallen nature, most of us extend our failure by trying to conceal our sins. When we do something wrong and hurtful, we hope to bury our toxic actions so no one will know. We cling to the false hope that if others don't know what we did, it won't be as bad. If we're really in denial, we sometimes try to pretend our mistake didn't happen at all. It's like pouring maple syrup in a car's gas tank, and then hiding the empty syrup bottle so that you won't be discovered. Your sticky sinfulness damages the car's fuel tank and capacity to operate, whether others know about it or not.

Adam and Eve set off a chain reaction that extends into the choices you and I make today. And clearly they aren't the only masqueraders mentioned in the Bible. We only have to look at the next generation, their children, to see another colossal sin cover-up. When God accepted Abel's offering but not Cain's, the second brother became jealous of the first. In a rage of fury, Cain killed his brother, Abel, on the spot.

Following the murder, Cain attempted to hide his sin from his all-knowing Father. Notice the exchange between God and Cain. "Then the Lord said to Cain, 'Where is your brother Abel?' 'I don't know,' he replied. 'Am I my brother's keeper?' " (Gen. 4:9). Can't you just see the way his eyes darted away? Or hear the hesitation in his voice? "Uh, what do you mean, God? I don't know what you're talking about. I have no idea where he is. Why are you asking me — do I look like Abel's babysitter?"

Someone sins; they cover it up; they deny it. The pattern continues. You may recall the story in Genesis about Joseph and the coat of many colors. When Joseph's brothers became jealous of him, they stripped him of his favored coat and threw him in the bottom of a pit. They considered killing him but decided instead to sell him into slavery.

Like so many others, the brothers devised a plan to cover their tracks. They went to great lengths to concoct a plausible story and contrive supporting evidence for their deceit. "Then they got Joseph's robe, slaughtered a goat and dipped the robe in the blood. They took the ornate robe back to their father and said, 'We found this. Examine it to see whether it is your son's robe' " (Gen. 37:31 – 32). In other words, "Hey, Dad, we think Joseph's gone, but we didn't do it." Notice that they don't even refer to Joseph as their brother here, but as their father's son. They were working hard to distance themselves from their responsibility.

Stop Hiding, Start Seeking

Hiding your sin might make life easier in the short run, but it always becomes worse over time. Proverbs 28:13 sums it up this way: "Whoever conceals their sins does not prosper, but the one who confesses and renounces them finds mercy." Those who hide their sins cannot receive God's blessings. Those who confess find mercy and forgiveness.

In your desire to cleanse your soul, you now stand at a crossroads. So far we've talked about facing the truth and overcoming the temptation to deceive oneself. We've examined the dangers of toxic words and thoughts, and how to overcome them both. As we move ahead, we'll look in depth at toxic emotions and how to transform them. We'll conclude our soul recovery plan by examining anything that might poison our relationship with God and by developing a preventive strategy for ongoing wholeness.

If you're serious about wanting to detoxify your soul, to experience a clean, fresh power in your Christian faith, then now is a good time to reflect on where you are with God, to examine your behavior with brutal honesty. What have you been hiding, perhaps even from yourself, that you need to face and bring before your Father?

Do you have a secret addiction? Do you struggle with porn, masturbation, or fantasy? Do you binge eat and then cover it up? Are you cutting — hurting yourself, then covering the scars? Are you shopping, spending, or gambling away your resources to numb your life's pain? Maybe it's the inconsistency between your intentions and your actions. Are you dishonoring God with your friends on Saturday night then going to church on Sunday like nothing happened? Are you going too far with your boyfriend or girlfriend? Stealing from your employer? Lying about your feelings to someone you love? Idolizing success or material possessions? Gossiping about your friends to make yourself look better?

Let me be blunt. You have a life-altering choice to make. Could it be that God put this book into your hands to lead you to do the right thing? Is it time to come out of hiding and get help for a sin you've been concealing? What will it be? Continuing to hide and cover your sin, hoping you'll never be found out? That's the easy road — at least in the short run. Or will you travel the more difficult road — the narrow way that leads to life — and confess your sin before God? If your heart's desire is to come clean, you will need to confess what has stained your soul.

If you choose to continue hiding, your sin may take you farther than you wanted to go and cost you more than you ever thought you'd pay. If you're willing to seek God's mercy and face the consequences with the people affected by your sin, you will experience more liberating joy than you ever thought imaginable. It's time to stop hiding and start seeking.

Ripped from the Headlines

In our pattern of sin, cover-up, and denial, there's a fourth element. In fact, you could call it the inevitable outcome of these three deadly ingredients — disclosure. Our secrets always come to light one way or another. It's just a matter of time before the garment of deception that we've woven with our lies comes unraveled, leaving the truth naked for everyone to see.

And it doesn't matter who you are, how powerful you may be, or how much money you have to wallpaper over your sin. In a story that sounds like it belongs in a celebrity gossip tabloid more than in the Bible, we find one of the most devious conspiracies of all time.

Consider some of the possible headlines: "Royal Scandal with Bathing Beauty! King's Married Lover Pregnant! Soldier Killed So King Can Marry Widow!"

King David was described as "a man after God's own heart" (see 1 Sam. 13:14). Even though he passionately loved his heavenly Father, like us, David was not immune to temptation. A single glance ignited a powder keg of adultery, murder, and conspiracy that exploded into every area of this king's life:

> In the spring, at the time when kings go off to war, David sent Joab out with the king's men and the whole Israelite army. They destroyed the Ammonites and besieged Rabbah. But David remained in Jerusalem.
>
> One evening David got up from his bed and walked around on the roof of the palace. From the roof he saw a woman bathing. The woman was very beautiful, and David sent someone to find out about her. The man said, "She is Bathsheba, the daughter of Eliam and the wife of Uriah the Hittite." Then David sent messengers to get her. She came to him, and he slept with her.... Then she went back home. The woman conceived and sent word to David, saying, "I am pregnant."
>
> — 2 Samuel 11:1 – 5

At the beginning of the story, you'll notice that it was spring, a time when kings traditionally went to the battlefront if their nation was at war, but King David stayed in Jerusalem. You could say David was not where he was supposed to be, so he saw something he wasn't supposed to see, then he did something he wasn't supposed to do, and it cost him more than he ever planned to pay. Being in the wrong place never helps you to do the right thing.

David discovered this truth in the flesh — literally — when "from the roof he saw a woman bathing." It sounds innocent enough, but the original language gives us more insight. The word translated as "saw" is much more vivid than our English translation captures. It comes from the Hebrew word *ra'ah* and means "to gaze, to stare, or to look intently." A variation of this word refers to a bird of prey, such as a vulture, that has amazing vision with which to swoop and prey on an unlucky creature. In other words, David didn't just see her. He was checking her out and liking what he saw.

Our heroic but all-too-human king succumbed to what the Bible calls the "lust of the flesh" or the "desires of the sinful nature." (See 1 John 2:16 and Gal. 5:16.) The enemy of our souls tempts us with different kinds of sins to pull us away from God and destroy our lives. The lusts of the flesh are some of the most difficult for many people to overcome. It seems like the body's desires overwhelm the logic of the brain and erode the power of the will.

Perhaps the battle within David went something like this: "I know this isn't a good idea. I shouldn't do this. I shouldn't keep looking at her. There's no way it will end well." But the desires of his body shut down his brain and stamped DENIED across the application of his willpower. "Keep logic out of this. She looks amazing. I want her. I'm the king! And I'm going to have her."

For many, lust overwhelms the mind and takes the body prisoner.

Some people struggle similarly when it comes to eating. The mind says no, but the body says yes. For others it may be alcohol, drugs, or cigarettes. Logically, we know that smoking or drinking isn't good for us, but the body decides to get what it wants.

The Not-So-Amazing Spider-Man

Perhaps Sir Walter Scott, the Scottish poet and novelist, had David in mind when he wrote, "Oh what a tangled web we weave, / When first we practice to deceive!" Because once David found out that Bathsheba was going to have his baby, he immediately began spinning a web that would put Spider-Man to shame. And when one plan didn't stick, David spun another direction and tried again.

Plan A: Bring Bathsheba's husband, Uriah, back from the war. Spending the night at home with his wife, surely they'd share a little wine, listen to some Luther Vandross, and nine months later, Uriah would assume the baby was his.

Unfortunately for David, when Uriah came home, he refused to dishonor his troops by enjoying his wife and instead slept outside the palace (see 2 Sam. 11:6 – 11).

Plan B: Get Uriah drunk and watch his noble valor fall by the wayside. Sounds like a logical plan, but once again, even three sheets to the wind, Uriah slept outside his house to honor God and his men (see 2 Sam. 11:12 – 13).

Plan C: Send Uriah back to the war, put him on the front lines, and pray he gets killed in battle (see 2 Sam. 11:14 – 15).

Finally, a plan that worked. Uriah, a man of great honor who did nothing wrong, was killed in battle. Many times, we're tempted to take similar measures — not leading to murder, I hope, but nonetheless conniving and wrong — to hide our sins from those around us. We don't want to risk losing our reputation, status, material possessions, or other relationships because of what we've done. So we start spinning sticky webs.

Plan A: You erase the history on your iPhone, iPad, or laptop, hoping no one discovers the sites you've visited. Or you hide the bottle so no one knows what pills you popped or drinks you drank. You bury the wrappers, packages, or jugs from all the candy, chips, and ice cream you devoured.

Plan B: If you get caught, lie. Deflect. Make up a wild story involving "a friend" who's addicted to whatever the evidence would indicate. You're really trying to help this friend, but it's so hard when she's in such pain and denial. Oh, this isn't something you would ever do, just your friend. You're innocent as long as you don't change your story.

Plan C: If plan B doesn't work, play the victim. Blame the other person, or your spouse, or your kids, or your parents, or your pastor, or your congressman. Shout. Tell the person that if they had been doing what they were supposed to be doing, then you wouldn't have done what you did. Whatever you do, don't take responsibility for your own sins.

No matter how hard you try, you are not hiding from God. Jesus said, "For there is nothing hidden that will not be disclosed, and nothing concealed that will not be known or brought out into the open"

(Luke 8:17). No matter how clever we think we are at hiding, God sees through our games. If the previous warning is not sobering enough, consider this promise: "You may be sure that your sin will find you out" (Num. 32:23). Whether today, tomorrow, next week, next month, next year, next decade, or the life to come, your sin *will* come out. You cannot hide forever.

Isn't it time to come clean?

Day of Reckoning

We know from Scripture that God disciplines those he loves (see Prov. 3:12). He knew that the unconfessed sin festering in David's soul needed to be released and washed away. So God mercifully sent the prophet Nathan to confront, correct, and help David do what's right.

Here's my version of their conversation (from 2 Sam. 12:5–6):

Nathan said, "David, I want to tell you a story. Once upon a time there were two men. One was filthy rich and had more lambs than you could count. The other was dirt poor and had only one lamb. The poor man raised the lamb and treated him as a pet. One day a beggar came asking for some food. The rich guy took the poor guy's pet lamb and killed it to give to the beggar."

David shouted, "As surely as the Lord lives, the man who did this must die! He must pay for that lamb four times over, because he did such a thing and had no pity."

The mighty king had no idea that he'd been set up. Nathan looked him straight in the eyes and said, "*You* are the man!"

Who Wants to Know?

Maybe in his mercy, God will show you, like Nathan showed David, that "you are the man!" or "you are the woman!" You've been hiding toxic behavior, and it's time to make it right. In order to make things right, you need to consider two types of confession. Both are integral for different reasons. We must confess to God. And then we must confess to other people.

Let's start with confession to God. We confess to God because we need his forgiveness. And the amazing story of his grace through Christ is that there is no sin too dark for his light. There is no sin too gross for his grace. There is no sin you have committed that God will not forgive when you confess to him and turn from your sin.

The Bible says, "If we confess our sins, he is faithful and just and will forgive us our sins and purify us from all unrighteousness" (1 John 1:9).

Repentance is the word used in the Bible for sincere confession. *Re* means "to turn back." *Pent* means "that which is highest," like a penthouse. When someone repents, he turns back to God's highest way of living instead of the lower ways of sin.

It is important to note that there is a vast difference between remorse and repentance. Often times, if someone is caught, they feel remorse: "I wish I didn't get caught." Repentance is more than sorrow for being caught. It is a deep sorrow for choosing our own route instead of God's. It's ownership of how you have hurt others with your own selfishness.

When Nathan confronted David, the king finally did the right thing. More than just being sorry he was caught, he repented to God for his sin. We looked briefly at a portion of Psalm 51 earlier. Some people don't realize that David wrote this psalm after recognizing his sin with Bathsheba. Consider the depth of emotion crying out from his heart as you read these words: "Have mercy on me, O God, according to your unfailing love; according to your great compassion blot out my transgressions. Wash away all my iniquity and cleanse me from my sin … Create in me a pure heart, O God, and renew a steadfast spirit within me. Do not cast me from your presence or take your Holy Spirit from me. Restore to me the joy of your salvation and grant me a willing spirit, to sustain me" (Ps. 51:1 – 2, 10 – 12).

Can you hear his heart's cry? You might pray a similar prayer in a spirit of repentance. I know I have several times. "Have mercy on me! I don't deserve your forgiveness and I know I can't earn it, but I humbly ask you to forgive my sins. Wash away all my filth and guilt. My heart has been so impure. Please, God, make my heart new again. Give me a willing spirit to do what pleases you and not to give in to my flesh. Help me fall in love with you like I just met you for the first time."

Maybe now is the time to pray this to God.

If you do, then you must also know that God says you are forgiven. He does not remember your sins (Isa. 43:25). He throws them into the sea of forgetfulness (Mic. 7:19). He doesn't remember them anymore. They are as far from you as the east is from the west (Ps. 103:12). Hear God's voice echo deep in your spirit.

You are forgiven.

The Other Half of Confession

Let me warn you. Confessing to God is the easier part of the two-fold confession that cleanses you from the toxic residues of sin. God already knows your sin anyway, so you might as well talk to him about it. However, other people don't know unless you tell them or they discover it themselves.

This second aspect of confession takes more courage. Not only should we confess to God, but we also have to confess to people. The purpose of confessing to people is much different from why we confess to God. We confess our sins to God for forgiveness. But we confess our sins to people for healing. James says clearly, "Therefore confess your sins to *each other* and pray for each other so that *you may be healed*" (5:16, emphases mine). When we confess to and pray for one another, we find healing from God through his people.

Now, we don't have to confess everything to everybody, and you should use discernment about who truly needs to know. But don't hide behind the lie that you're "protecting others" by withholding your confession from them. Pray about who has been affected by your sin. Ask God to show you who can help with your healing, a faith-filled friend or mentor, a more mature believer or pastor.

Whenever someone confesses to me, "I'm about to tell you something I've never told anyone," I know this person is about to make a breakthrough. He or she may have confessed to God countless times a problem, sin, or need, but when that person confesses to another person, something different starts to happen.

You might be tempted to think, "I can just confess my sin to

God — that's all I need to do." If your goal is forgiveness only, then you are right. But if you'd like strength and encouragement to overcome falling into the same sinful trap, remember our loving God loves to work through his people. As I implied earlier, if you are trapped in a habitual sin, chances are good you need God's help through his people.

Stripped Clean

Several years ago at our church, I witnessed these principles acted out in a life-altering way. I had just taught a similar message to our church about the power of dropping our masks and uncovering our sins to God and other people. That Sunday night, a single man confessed openly to the men and women in his small group that he'd been praying about a problem for years, but he'd never told another person. Choking back tears, he humbly admitted that he struggled with an addiction to pornography.

That night, a young lady I'll call Marla was participating in the group for the first time. She was a brand new Christian and very nervous to be a part of a small group Bible study. She told me later that the moment the guy confessed his sin, she could barely catch her breath. She was certain the group would turn on him.

What happened next helped Marla to make a pivotal decision that changed the direction of her life. After the guy confessed his lustful problem, instead of looking down on him, everyone in the group embraced him. Another guy talked openly about his past struggles with pornography. Then a woman in the group shared that porn had gripped her during one season of life too. She explained how Christ and her friends had helped her overcome it. Each person encouraged the guy in their own way, and then everyone joined hands and prayed passionately for their brother in Christ.

Seeing firsthand the unconditional love and acceptance moved Marla to take a risk. Trembling with emotion, she explained to her newfound spiritual family that she'd gotten pregnant in high school and the father of her baby skipped out, leaving her to raise her son by herself. Struggling to make ends meet, she'd taken a job as an exotic dancer. She despised her job and knew it was wrong, but the money was good and paid the bills. She'd give anything to quit her degrading job but felt trapped with no way out.

That's when a chain reaction of miracles started to unfold. Just as when the guy confessed his sin, the group expressed to Marla the same love and acceptance. A group member boldly told her, "If you quit your job, I'll give you money to help cover the bills." Like the closing scene from *It's a Wonderful Life* when everyone brings George Bailey money to help in his time of need, everyone in the group started pledging financial help. Within minutes, the small group committed enough money to last her a couple of months.

Marla couldn't believe what was happening. It was as if God himself reached down and hugged her through his people. The next day, the emboldened follower of Christ marched into the club where she worked and told the manager she was finished and never coming back.

On Tuesday, one of the small group members pulled a favor from a friend and got Marla an interview at his company. The manager liked Marla, and on Wednesday, because of God's goodness through his children, Marla started a new job and a new life.

Marla could have confessed her sin to God and been forgiven. But when she confessed to God's people, she found healing. Now she is helping other girls find the same freedom she knows. Armed with God's Spirit and the strength of his family, Marla launched a ministry to help other girls escape the stripping industry.

If you've been living a toxic lie, hiding sins from others, it's time to drop your guard and invite others to help. Confess to God. He sent Jesus to die for your sins. He wants to forgive you. But don't stop there. Take the next step and confess to God's people. Do it. Experience the healing power of love through God's people. Rather than sinking into the quicksand of sin, you can swim in the clean water of God's forgiveness and cleansing love.

Part 2

TOXIC EMOTIONS

5

Bitter Roots

Digging Up the Destructive Source of Resentment

Bitterness is like a cancer. It eats upon the host.

—Maya Angelou

One of the things I love about having six kids is watching how they stick up for each other. While they're more than willing to go ten rounds at home over who gets the last blueberry waffle, at soccer practice or playgroup or, yes, even at church, they defend the Groeschel name with a fierceness that belongs in *Braveheart*. Growing up, I was the same way with my sister. Even though I could harass her for fun, if someone else messed with her, I'd defend her to the death.

It's not surprising then that my biggest struggle with bitterness started when my family discovered the awful truth about someone we had trusted in a position of authority over my little sister. I've written previously about this very sick man, whom I called Max, but the memory of what he did still haunts me. Most kids in our small town junior high school took at least one class from Max on their journey through the sixth grade. To many kids, Max was a favorite teacher — always cutting up, telling jokes, and handing out easy A's. To me, he became the object of the deepest bitterness that I've ever known.

Throughout the years, Max developed special relationships with his favorite students. Though none of us were aware at the time, we discovered years later that all his favorite students "happened" to be cute, young girls. My little sister, whom I treasured and loved, became one of Max's victims.

The day I found out that Max had molested my little sister remains one of the most disturbing, surreal times of my life. At first, I didn't want to believe it. It couldn't be true. Not Max. Not my sister! Unfortunately, she wasn't his only victim. Girl after girl recounted similar stories of how Max had sexually abused them. Painfully, we learned that this twisted teacher carefully selected his victims, showered them with presents, and lured them into his trap. The once beloved teacher had created an extensive collection of lives shattered by his unholy desires.

Some studies show that as many as one out of three girls and one in four boys suffer some sort of sexual abuse. Whatever the numbers, this tragedy must crush God's heart. I know it crushed mine as a brother.

As I'm typing these words, I'm tearing up thinking about what these sweet girls endured. God only knows how many suffered as Max pleasured himself at their expense. I remember trying to absorb the painful truth. How should I respond? Should we track him down? Have him arrested? Beat the life out of him?

Make no mistake; I was furious the moment that I heard about his abuse. But the more I thought about it, my anger blossomed into rage. The seed of bitterness planted in my heart grew to a full-blown briar patch of revenge. I prayed that Max would suffer eternally in hell, and I vowed to make him suffer on earth before facing God's judgment.

My plan for revenge wasn't necessary. To my bittersweet delight, we later found that Max was suffering in a hospital, fighting for his life against a crippling disease, muscular dystrophy. I remember thanking God for his justice in giving Max what he deserved.

The Root of the Problem

Most would agree that my bitterness toward Max was justifiable. After what he did to my sister (and his other victims), who could blame me for being angry? No matter how justifiable my feelings were, however, in God's eyes my self-righteous hatred was just as sinful as Max's crime. Even writing that statement all these years later remains difficult — how could my desire for justice be considered as sinful as this monster's lustful actions? The vast majority of people would agree that my hate and judgmental rage were more than justified.

In the course of time, however, I learned that bitterness never draws us closer to God. Bitterness is a nonproductive, toxic emotion, usually resulting from resentment over unmet needs. I was angry that my family could not hurt Max in return for what he stole from my sister. My unmet need was not only for justice but for retribution; I wanted him to suffer, to live with the awful awareness of the kind of man he was and what he did.

Instead, I was punishing no one but myself and those around me who experienced the scalding spillovers of the acid churning inside me. My self-induced misery led only to a chain reaction. Like a master criminal needing support for a big heist, bitterness never works alone. Its insidious partners include jealousy, anger, hatred, disobedience, contempt, gossip, rage, and countless other tag-alongs. The job they're planning is to rob anyone they can of peace, hope, joy, forgiveness, and mercy. Instead of just inflicting one cut on our souls, bitterness and its gang litter our spiritual path with layers of crushed glass, leaving us to bleed a slow, agonizing death of resentful rage.

God's Word shows us clearly the dangers of bitterness: "Make every effort to live in peace with everyone and to be holy; without holiness no one will see the Lord. See to it that no one falls short of the grace of God and that *no bitter root grows up to cause trouble and defile many*" (Heb. 12:14 – 15, emphasis mine). Though we can't control the outcome, we're called to do everything possible to live at peace with others, even those — or *especially* those — who have hurt us. The problem is that when you're filled with bitterness, as I was with Max, you don't want to believe this verse applies to your situation — but it does. The writer to the Hebrews warns us to be on guard for the root of bitterness.

We must watch for it and do everything possible to fight against it. If we're not careful, if we allow bitterness to take root in our lives, then we might miss God's grace in our lives. Why? Because the root of bitterness defiles and poisons.

Bitterness works underground, slithering beneath the surface. No one can see the poison coursing through your veins. On the outside you might look normal. You can fool others for a while. But on the inside, our bitterness starts to boil. "I can't believe she did that to me. I wouldn't treat my worst enemy that way." "I am so angry I could kill someone. He's going to pay for this, one way or another."

Over time, our bitterness poisons our hearts. "I wouldn't be surprised if something really bad happens to him. He deserves it, you know." "If I ever see her, there is no telling what I might do." "I pray that God gives him what he really deserves."

I pray you've never experienced something like my family did with Max. If you have, then you know too well the tempting knock of bitterness on the door of your heart. Unfortunately, if you've lived for long, you've experienced some sort of pain or betrayal. Perhaps someone that you love suffered abuse. Or maybe you were that someone. You might have had a close friend that gossiped about you or betrayed a confidence. You thought you could trust them, but their unfaithfulness proved you wrong. Maybe someone didn't stand up for you when you know they should have covered your back. You now wonder whom you can trust. Perhaps you tried to help someone and they took advantage of your generosity. Or maybe a close business partner lied to you and cheated you. Or you might have put your trust in another Christian, who then did something to you that didn't represent Christ at all.

If you are not on guard, a root of bitterness can grow in the soil of a hurt that hasn't been dealt with properly. It's obviously not a sin on your part when someone hurts you. But if you don't handle the hurt properly, their sin becomes a catalyst for your own. Then you won't be hurt once, but hurt twice or even more. That's what happened to me as I stewed over Max. The more I imagined what he'd done, the deeper bitterness grew its roots into the soil of my heart. And the more its flagrant poison infiltrated my soul.

Poison Blooms

At one time or another, each of us must contend with the stench of someone else's sin and decide how we will respond to it. I'll never forget the devastating seeds of destruction that took root and bloomed in one couple's marriage. Michelle was the mother of two sons and married to a spiritually growing Christian man named Tony. Everything seemed perfect to Michelle until the day Tony confessed to her his secret sin. When Tony was thirteen years old, he found a stash of pornographic magazines that lured him into a trap that he couldn't escape. At first, he didn't see any harm in just looking. After all, he wasn't hurting anyone. But his curiosity soon became an unbreakable habit that turned into a lifelong addiction. When Tony became a Christian a year before his marriage, he realized that he shouldn't look lustfully. Unfortunately, porn had him tightly within its grip. As hard as he tried, Tony couldn't stop looking. He managed to cover his tracks but couldn't cover his guilt.

After over two decades of hiding his sin, Tony decided that enough was enough and he decided to come clean with his wife. Through tears he begged for her forgiveness and asked her if she'd help him. Based on my experience, Tony did the right thing. In most relationships, confession generally leads to some short-term challenges but long-term healing. Instead, Michelle threw her alarm clock at him as hard as she could, called him several names, and moved out of their house and in with her mom.

"I hate his guts!" Michelle shouted at me when I saw her for the first time since learning of Tony's addiction. Then she burst into tears. Since I had just spent an hour with her husband, I knew exactly where he stood. I knew it would be a hard road back to trust, but because Tony was deeply repentant, with work, prayer, and counseling, I felt confident he could overcome his addiction and they could have an even better marriage than they did before.

When Michelle told me she was leaving him, I assumed she spoke out of her hurt and that she'd cool over time. My assumption was wrong. Michelle let Satan plant a seed of bitterness in her heart that grew into a mature tree of hatred. Day after day, she stewed, imagining the filthy images her husband viewed. Rather than moving closer toward forgiveness, she moved deeper into resentment.

As the bitter root grew, Michelle decided the only way to get back at her husband was to put him through the same pain that he'd caused her. So she dressed up in her sexiest dress, one that showed off all her curves, and headed to the most popular bar in town. It didn't take long for her to draw attention from a man. That night she went to his place and spent the night with a guy she'd just met. Her bitterness had turned into acid, searing her heart and numbing her conscience.

One bad decision led to another, and Michelle's life spiraled out of control. What I hoped would be a marriage on the road to healing became a marriage in a head-on collision with hatred. Sadly, their marriage quickly disintegrated into an ugly divorce. Today, Michelle remains convinced all men are evil even though she continues to hop from one to another. There is no question that Tony's sin started the problem. But Michelle's choice of bitterness rather than forgiveness turned their shared problem into irresolvable heartache.

Fruit Loops

All roots, whether those of a giant Redwood or of personal bitterness, sustain themselves by what they absorb and the direction they grow. The roots absorb whatever moisture is nearby into their system to nourish the tree. If the roots absorb clean water, the tree will grow strong and healthy. If the roots absorb contaminated water, the tree becomes diseased and unhealthy. Just like people. The more they dwell on a hurt, the more poison their hearts absorb.

Roots also grow deep. A corrupted root sinks itself deep into the ground, making the tree or plant extremely difficult to remove. So too a root of bitterness locks a person in place and makes it hard for them to move forward in life. If the roots multiply and become entangled, they can choke the life out of you.

Jesus said, "A good tree cannot bear bad fruit, and a bad tree cannot bear good fruit" (Matt. 7:18). What makes a tree good or bad? The source is often found in the root. What does a bitter root produce? Poisonous fruit. The New Living Translation renders Hebrews 12:15 this way: "Watch out that no poisonous root of bitterness grows up to trouble you, corrupting many." The word in the Greek translated as "defile" or "corrupt" is *miaino*. It means "to stain, to pollute, or to contaminate."

The more I meditated on Max's actions to my sister, the more polluted and contaminated my soul became. I became obsessed with making sure he paid for his wrongdoings. And guess whom my bitterness hurt the most?

Me.

A little bitterness goes a long way. Add a little bitterness to any environment and watch it suffer. A few bitter teens can derail a whole youth group. A couple of bitter moms can poison a PTA board. A bitter deacon can split a church.

You've probably noticed that one bitter person can destroy morale in a work environment. A little griping here, some more complaining there, add some backbiting and gossip, and your workplace becomes hell on earth.

Bitterness can also destroy a family faster than you can say, "Pop goes the weasel." Take any family betrayal: a divorce, a broken promise, an addiction, a misunderstanding. Let the problem divide people into two sides. Force them to pick one. And you've got a problem that could divide a family for a lifetime.

Bitterness never produces good results. Because a person's been hurt, they often justify their bitterness. If they are cruel or angry to another, they feel completely justified. "I only feel this way because of what she did to me. She has this coming."

The bitter person quickly becomes overly critical. The Bible says that love keeps no record of wrongs. But bitterness keeps detailed records. Looking through a lens of hurt, all bitter people can do is find fault. "I can't believe he acts that way. Who does he think he is?" They may even secretly celebrate another person's misfortunes. When something bad happens, they simply believe this person had it coming.

It's not uncommon for someone to write off a whole group of people. A betrayed man thinks all women are deceivers. A disappointed person decides all Christians are hypocrites. An abused child might decide you can't trust any adult.

The problem is that many bitter people don't know they are bitter. Since they are so convinced that they are right, they can't see their own wrong in the mirror. And the longer the root of bitterness grows, the more difficult it is to remove.

Roto-Rooter

We had a big problem with roots growing into the lines running from our toilets out to our septic tank. (Gross, I know.) Several times a year, I'd have to call a company to come unclog the lines. Finally the problem got so old and costly, we decided to remove the tree causing the problems and dig up the roots.

If you are dealing with bitterness, you'll have to do something similar. The only way to remove bitterness from your life is to kill it at its root. And there is only one way to kill the root of bitterness: with forgiveness. Ephesians 4:31 – 32 says, "Get rid of all bitterness, rage and anger, brawling and slander, along with every form of malice. Be kind and compassionate to one another, *forgiving each other*, just as in Christ God forgave you" (emphasis mine).

Growing up, I was taught to treat other people as you want to be treated. Paul takes this good advice and makes it godly advice. He doesn't say to treat others as you want to be treated; instead he says to treat others as Christ treated you. In other words, forgive in the same way that you've been forgiven.

When I became a Christian, I carried over my deep-rooted bitterness toward Max. Even though as a new Christian I started to learn the principles of forgiveness, I rationalized that Max was the exception to God's command to forgive. Surely God wouldn't require me to forgive someone who did something as horrible as Max did to those girls.

Unfortunately, I learned that God's command to forgive doesn't have exceptions. To make matters more challenging for my bitter heart, I discovered these words of Jesus: "For if you forgive other people when they sin against you, your heavenly Father will also forgive you. But if you do not forgive others their sins, your Father will not forgive your sins" (Matt. 6:14 – 15). Let me highlight the words of Christ, just in case you breezed by them the first time. If you don't forgive others, God will not forgive you. Whoa.

I remember arguing with God. "How can I forgive someone who did something so horrible? I don't want to forgive. Max deserves to pay." Though the memories of Max's abuse continued to haunt me, so did Christ's command to forgive.

Over time and after lots of prayer, I finally surrendered to the idea that forgiving the man who'd hurt my sister was the right and biblical thing to do. Even though I knew it was right, that didn't make it any easier.

I started by trying to pray for Max. You'd think that praying for someone else would never be hard. I don't know if I've ever done anything more difficult. "Bless Max," I prayed half-heartedly, not meaning one of the two words I prayed. That was a start.

I've found that your prayers for others may or may not change them, but they always change you. As I tried sincerely to pray for a betrayer, slowly my bitter root started to die. To be honest, I don't think I even noticed it at first. But the poison that I'd been allowing into my heart started to subside.

Shaken Up

In more than twenty years of ministry, I can't think of a more tragic event that would justify a bitter spirit. However, I may have never observed a better picture of God's grace and forgiveness than through two couples that had to work through an unbearable offense.

Two young wives I'll call Jeanette and Suzy were inseparable. They enjoyed studying the Bible weekly with two other couples, they took family outings together, and they raised their kids together.

When Jeanette decided to take a part-time job for some extra money, Suzy offered to watch her newborn daughter. They all felt blessed by a win-win situation until one day, Jeanette's eighteen-month-old daughter stopped breathing in bed. Panicking as any mom would, Jeanette dialed 911, praying while trying to keep breathing herself. Thankfully the medical professionals revived the toddler and rushed her to the hospital, where the doctor explained that an X-ray revealed trauma to the toddler's head. To make matters worse, the doctor expressed concerns that this injury could cause permanent damage to the brain and suggested that someone had purposely injured the child.

Accusations started to fly. Various people got involved praying and asking questions. No one thought that Jeanette would hurt her own child, and Suzy, her close friend, couldn't be a suspect, could she?

The state authorities had to be involved for the sake of the little girl, and things quickly devolved from bad to worse. Everyone became a suspect. Because no one knew where to place the blame, the authorities removed all the children from both Jeanette and Suzy's homes. When the doctors acknowledged that there would be lasting damage, reality set in. Someone abused a child, and the damage was real and lasting.

Jeanette became convinced that her friend Suzy had hurt her daughter. Suzy stood her ground. With a line in the sand, even neutral friends starting picking sides. Hurt turned to bitterness. And the root started to grow — deeper than you can imagine.

After almost two years, the case was finally closed. That's when Suzy shocked everyone. Against her lawyer's advice, she confessed to injuring Jeanette's daughter. She didn't mean to do it, but she did. Though she could have kept the incident a secret and no one would have ever known, after her confession, a judge sentenced her to jail for 712 days — one day for every day that she didn't confess her crime.

Grace Notes

Healing can take place if we have the courage to forgive. A few years ago, I preached a message on bitterness and the power of forgiveness to kill bitter roots. With permission from my sister, who is a part of our church, I shared her story of the abuse she endured from Max. Thankfully, my sister now helps other girls heal from similar pain.

In the message, I explained how bitterness hurts the bitter person the most. I shared the same verses on forgiveness that I've written about in this chapter. Then I told how God changed my heart.

The same time I started the process of forgiving Max, his body took a turn for the worse. His muscular dystrophy got the upper hand, and we got word that Max didn't have long to live.

By the miraculous power of God, my sister, our parents, and I decided to forgive Max for his wrongdoing. God had freely forgiven us. How could we withhold the same grace from someone else?

I sent a note to Max while he was under hospice care, preparing to die in his home. In the note, I wrote over drops of tears how Christ had forgiven and changed me. I explained that God wanted to do the same thing for Max. As simply as I could, I told the story of the gospel, highlighting the grace and forgiveness possible through Christ.

After Max's funeral, I found out the nurse caring for him read him the note, and Max gave his life to Christ. Even though Max certainly doesn't deserve it, he will spend eternity forgiven by God in heaven. As much as that doesn't seem fair to me, my story is not so dissimilar. Even though I never molested anyone, I've sinned grievously against my holy God. I, just like Max, will spend eternity forgiven by God in heaven, even though I don't deserve it.

After telling that story to our church, I watched miracle after miracle as people decided to forgive those who had hurt them and let go of the bitterness that hurt them even more. Although we shouldn't have underestimated the power of God's grace and forgiveness, no one was more shocked than I was when it became clear that Suzy and Jeanette's story was not over. After Suzy served her jail time, she and her husband visited Jeanette and her husband in their home. In tears, Suzy fell on her knees and asked for forgiveness. And Jeanette and her husband freely forgave Suzy for injuring their daughter, who was now four years old. Although this little girl is as cute as a kid can be, she'll always walk with a limp and battle a speech impediment resulting from the injury. After the apology, Jeanette and her husband asked Suzy if she wanted to hold their daughter. As you can imagine, no one had a dry eye at that meeting. Bitterness left. Healing came. And no one who knows their story can stay the same.

Act When You Can

There's a reason God wants us to love and pray for our enemies and those who have wronged us. He could have told us to let time heal the wound a bit, or to take it easy until we're ready to move on. Instead, we're told to pray sooner. Like, now.

Even after all God taught me with Max, I still had to relearn the lesson the hard way. Before I started Life Church, I was an associate pastor at a church in Oklahoma City. One of the pastors there became a mentor to me. Like a coach, he encouraged me to do things in ministry I never thought I could do. Before long, he and his wife became close and trusted friends to my family.

Sadly, my friend made some costly mistakes that hurt many people and cost him his job as a pastor. Even though he left his role at our church and moved to another state, we remained close friends. Knowing his tenderness toward God, I prayed constantly that his family would heal and that one day he'd be restored to ministry.

Two years later we started Life Church, and he asked if he could join my staff. Sensing he had more healing to experience, I invited him to serve faithfully as a volunteer for a year, and then we could talk about a staff position. My friend moved his family back to our city and took a job just so he could serve at our church.

I was counting down the days, hoping to hire him at the end of the year. His gifts were a perfect complement to mine. Our church loved him, and he loved our church. However, my friend began to make bad decisions again. When I confronted him, hoping to help, he used me as a verbal punching bag to unload years of hurt.

When we parted ways that day, I was dazed by what had just happened. Beyond a shadow of a doubt, my friend was hurting and in some kind of trouble. He'd obviously made decisions that would hurt those who loved him most again. Perhaps it was out of embarrassment, shame, or anger. Whatever the reason, he pushed me and others who loved him away.

Believing we'd work through this as we'd worked through challenges before, I decided to give him room to breathe. Days turned into weeks as I continued to work at church. I prayed consistently for my friend, but I didn't contact him. One evening I was preaching a message on reconciling relationships. In the middle of the message, I realized I needed to reach out to him. On the way home, I told my wife that I would call him the next day.

That chance never came. When I got home, my answering

machine had a message from my friend's wife. She had found him hanging dead from a rafter in his garage.

Four days later, I performed my friend's funeral. Hundreds of stunned friends and family members gathered as we buried the man we loved so much. Even though I know his death wasn't my fault, for the remainder of my life I'll regret that I didn't reach out.

Life is uncertain. Eternity is not. Unforgiveness cannot be allowed to last another day. Are you holding a grudge? You will never be more like God than when you forgive. Let it go. Kill the root of bitterness. Let the hurt go and set yourself free.

6

Green with Envy

Scratching the Poison Ivy of Comparison

*Envy is the art of counting the other fellow's blessings
instead of your own.*
—Harold Coffin

With six kids in our house, we've gone through seasons when certain issues seem to consume us — potty training, starting school, learning to ride a bike without training wheels. Each new chapter gets multiplied times six. There was a period when someone always had a loose tooth, and it seemed like teeth were going to be falling out forever. The tooth fairy was coming around more than our mailman.

If you know anything about me, it's possible you've heard that I tend to be, ahem, rather "conservative" financially. I can own that.

God has made me much more generous as I've gotten older, but in those days, the going rate for the tooth fairy at our house was one American dollar.

Maybe the economy was better at some of your houses, or maybe it had something to do with inflation. But one day, my little Anna, who was seven at the time and had just received a crisp dollar bill for a baby molar, came running to me, obviously upset. "Daddy! Daddy! You're not gonna *believe* this! You know how we get a *dollar* from our tooth fairy? My friend McKae said her tooth fairy brings her *five* dollars!" My poor daughter was beside herself, as distraught as any investor would be watching her portfolio shrink before her very eyes.

She wondered aloud, "Daddy, why, why, why? It just isn't fair! How come we only get a dollar when McKae gets five?"

My mind raced to come up with an acceptable explanation. Fortunately, my little girl came to my rescue as she continued to think out loud. "Daddy, maybe we can find out which tooth fairy they use and just switch to theirs!"

Let Me Have It

It's not just kids wanting to switch to more affluent tooth fairies. At one time or another, all of us want what others have that we don't. This personal scrutiny in which we compare where we stand in the world with where we see others is usually distilled into the word *envy*. From the Old French word *envie*, which in turn originated in the Latin word *invidia*, it literally means "to look upon with malice or resentment." Its closest kin include discontentment, dissatisfaction, and covetousness, all born of the marriage of comparison and resentment.

We see what someone else has, and we want it for ourselves. If we think that we deserve the object of our desire more than the person who has it, our envy blossoms into jealousy. In either case, we're polluting our souls with spores of discontentment that will bloom into lust, avarice, and greed. Put simply, envy is when you resent God's goodness in other people's lives and ignore God's goodness in your own life. It's when you think, "They've got it and I want it. They don't even deserve it. They shouldn't have it in the first place!"

Our consumer culture thrives on envy. Don't you wish you had the latest iToy? Or a new car with leather interior that can park itself or be started electronically from miles away? Or a newer house in a better neighborhood? Or a better vacation destination? If we took every ad and commercial seriously, we'd never have one moment of satisfaction in our lives. We could never enjoy what we have because we'd always be wanting what someone else has.

Despite what advertisers and pop psychologists tell us, we really can't have it all. If we're going to experience a clean, spiritual way of living, then like the apostle Paul we must learn to be "content in all things." We must learn to recognize envy in all its forms and have the antidote for its deadly poison close at hand.

I'll Have What She's Having

Like poisonous mushrooms or toxic mold spores, envy takes on a variety of forms. When many of us think of envy, we probably first associate it with materialism — money, possessions, toys. Even if we actually like our career, most of us can probably relate to wishing we had a better job, one in which we made more money. Is it just me, or does it seem like as soon as you get a car — whether it's new to you or brand new — the first time you drive it, you see a car you like better? Or if it's not car craving, it's boat bloat! All some guys want in life is a bigger bass boat. They're convinced that *then* they'd be happy.

Technology is the worst. As you're wheeling out of the store with the very newest, biggest, brightest, clearest TV, there's an employee from the warehouse wheeling in a newer, bigger, brighter, clearer one to put in the spot on the shelf you just emptied. And let's be honest: when it comes to technology, size matters. We want our TVs big and our phones small. It cracks me up that finally there's something in life that a guy actually wants smaller than the next guy's. Your friend takes out his new smart phone and you're like, "Man, that's amazing! I'd give anything for one that small."

Some people have appearance envy. One woman sees another woman and thinks, "Her figure is cuter than mine. Her chest is bigger and her hips are smaller than mine will ever be." Most women seem to wish some parts of their body were bigger while others were smaller. A lot of men feel similarly — about their hair. When a guy sees another guy with nicer, thicker hair than his, he wishes he had less hair on his back and more on his head!

Relational envy is another common one. Two single women may be very good friends. They hang out, they talk, they shop, and they're close. They have a great time together. Then one of them gets a boyfriend. At first, the woman without the boyfriend is happy for her friend. But inevitably, her loneliness begins to weigh heavier and heavier on her. It gets harder for her to celebrate her friend's happiness with sincerity. Her friend gets engaged and shows her the ring, all giddy and excited. She's polite and musters as much enthusiasm as she can but secretly thinks, "It's so not fair! Did you see how she flaunted that ring right in my face?"

Of course, married people experience their own virulent strain of envy. One woman just can't help noticing things about her friend's husband. He has a good job, he leads his family spiritually, he takes care of his body, he helps out around the house — he even gives the kids baths at night without being asked! Then she looks at her own husband, hunched down on the couch, watching a ball game, with a half-eaten bag of Doritos resting on his belly and orange crumbs on his beard and fingertips.

Husbands struggle with this too. A man notices that his friend's wife always seems to be encouraging her husband. She always backs him up, always brags on him, always has dinner ready, and never complains about taking care of the house. But it feels like every time his own wife opens her mouth, she's bossing him around, running him down, griping about something he hasn't done.

You know who I envy? People who have weekends off! I'm not kidding. What do I do on the weekends? Other than trying to save the souls of the world? Oh, not much ... I guess. And how does everyone else spend their weekends? They go to the lake. Go hiking. See a ballgame. Or sleep in. Or make blueberry pancakes. Sometimes I just feel like saying, "Okay, this weekend, everyone else can just go to hell. *I'm* going to the lake." (Just kidding.)

I also envy people whose jobs end at five o'clock. It feels like my job never ends. When many people leave the office and go home, their workday is over. As a pastor, I'm on call 24/7. I'm prone to envy having a "real" job — even though I know that I wouldn't be happy if I ate blueberry pancakes every morning and left the office at five on the dot every day. Envy is insatiable.

How about you? Who do you envy the most? Have you ever wished you had something or someone that you saw others enjoying? Maybe you're thinking, "Does it really matter if we want a little bit of something we don't have? We all do it, right? So what's the big deal?"

The Evils of Envy

The big deal is that allowing envy into your heart is like planting nuclear waste in your flowerbed. If you don't think envy is a serious problem, just consider what Scripture has to say about it. James doesn't mince words: "But if you harbor bitter envy and selfish ambition in your hearts, do not boast about it or deny the truth. Such 'wisdom' does not come down from heaven but is earthly, unspiritual, demonic. For where you have envy and selfish ambition, there you find disorder and every evil practice" (3:14 – 16). So this issue of being dissatisfied with what you have and instead wanting what others have isn't a big deal? "Every evil practice" sounds like a profoundly big deal to me.

We can find plenty of examples of envy throughout the Bible. In Genesis 4, Cain envied his brother Abel. God accepted Abel's offering, but he didn't accept Cain's. As a result of his envy, Cain's resentment festered into a poison possessing his heart and driving him to murder his brother. In Genesis 30, Rachel envied her sister Leah because Leah could bear children and she couldn't. Then later in the same chapter, they switched places, and it was Leah who envied Rachel.

In Genesis 37, Joseph's brothers envied him. Joseph was his father's favorite, and he kept having dreams and visions in which his brothers were bowing down to him. But instead of bowing, they decided it sounded like a better idea to beat him up, throw him in a pit, and sell him into slavery.

In 1 Samuel 18 we're told that mighty King Saul envied David, the shepherd boy turned warrior. The people made up a song with a not-so-sweet refrain about how Saul had slain his thousands but David his *tens* of thousands. Saul's jealousy eventually drove him crazy, literally, and he tried to pin David to the wall with a spear — twice. In the New Testament, in Mark 15, we find that Jesus himself was the subject of envy. Why was he handed over to the Roman authorities to be crucified? Because the chief priests *envied* him.

Jealousy, rage, bitterness, murder, and heart-wrenching grief — all emerging from the toxic power of envy.

Consider this: in Isaiah 14, Lucifer is said to have envied God, and consequently he rebelled and was cast out of heaven. We would do well to remember that envy is clearly the flint that ignites evil in our hearts. It apparently signals "I'm available" to demons searching for a cheap date. Envy is as volatile as nitroglycerin, and we cannot carry it inside us without evil exploding.

Proverbs 14:30 tells us that "a heart at peace gives life to the body, but envy rots the bones." The philosopher Socrates elaborates on this truth. He wrote, "Envy is the daughter of pride, the author of murder and revenge, the perpetual tormenter of virtue. Envy is the filthy slime of the soul, a venom, a poison which consumes the flesh and dries up the bones. It rots us like cancer from the inside."

No Comparison

So now we know it's earthly, unspiritual, and demonic to envy. But what can we do about it? The first thing is actually something that we can start *not* doing. Paul, in his letter to the Corinthians, writes, "We do not dare to classify or compare ourselves with some who commend themselves. When they measure themselves by themselves and compare themselves with themselves, they are not wise" (2 Cor. 10:12). Envy begins with comparison. And it's so easy, almost natural, to compare what we have (or lack) with those around us.

"They have a nicer car than I do, but I have a better house." It's so easy to rank ourselves against others. None of us are immune. In fact, you know who else did this? Jesus' disciples. The disciples were often comparing themselves with one another. Who's the most important? Who gets to sit by Jesus? Who's the greatest?

In John 21, Jesus has just restored Peter's position with him, commissioning him to "take care of my sheep." He prophesies about the kind of death Peter will die, and Peter asks, "What about John? What's going to happen to him?" Jesus answers, "What is that to you?" Essentially, he was saying, "Peter, that ain't none of your business!"

Just being honest, I occasionally struggle with comparing myself with other pastors. And when I do, it's never pretty. I should be content to just be who God called me to be. Several years ago, a ministry magazine ranked the fifty most influential pastors in the United States. I made that list. In fact, they ranked me in the top ten most influential. What an honor, right? There's somewhere between 385,000 and 400,000 senior pastors in the US. You'd be right to think, "Wow! You must have been thrilled."

I should have been. Unfortunately, my honest response was more like, "Really? Several are ranked higher than I am?" I'm extremely competitive, and it just bothered me. (One of our church members heard about it, and he later told me, with a smile, "I don't believe you were really on that list. You're not that good." I told him I'd pray for his soul while he was eating pancakes at the lake.)

Not only are these kinds of lists not particularly useful, they can actually bring out the worst in us. When we look at other people comparatively and competitively, we're not seeing them as our brothers and sisters. We're not loving them more than we love ourselves, and we're definitely not seeing them as God sees them. Romans 2 makes it clear that God doesn't show favoritism. His Word spells out that we shouldn't view people within hierarchies. Galatians 6:4 – 5 says, "Each one should test their own actions. Then they can take pride in themselves alone, *without comparing themselves to someone else*, for each one should carry their own load" (emphasis mine).

Ultimate Cage Fighting Grandma

I've suggested to you what *not* to do. First and foremost, guard against comparing yourself with others as much as possible. Train yourself not to use "better than" and "worse than" when thinking and talking about other people. When we see God's goodness in the lives of others, we shouldn't allow ourselves to feel resentful.

Now let's talk some about what *to* do. When we see God's goodness in the lives of others, we should feel joy. We should celebrate them, and we should celebrate *with* them. Romans 12:15 teaches us that we should "rejoice with those who rejoice; mourn with those who mourn."

You may not have realized it at the time, but if you've ever watched Ultimate Fighting or mixed martial arts, you've probably seen examples of this principle in practice. (If you don't know what Ultimate Fighting is, it's what Napoleon Dynamite's brother Kip was training for — to be a cage fighter. Rex Kwon Do!) Almost all of the competitors I've seen in Ultimate Fighting, no matter what happens in the ring — knuckles crunch, blood spills, bones break, eyes swell shut, it doesn't matter — when that match is over and the winner is declared, the other guy will genuinely congratulate him. They often even hug each other! The one who lost graciously acknowledges his opponent's success. And together they share a sense of celebration.

I actually learned this principle from my grandma. (I mean rejoicing with those who rejoice, not how to appreciate Ultimate Fighting.) Every Christmas, my grandma would send us two Christmas cards: my little sister Lisa would get a Christmas card with a check for twenty dollars, and I'd get a Christmas card with a check for twenty dollars. We were always so excited to get our cards from Grandma. But because Lisa's my little sister, of course it was my duty — my spiritual responsibility — to mess with her. Lisa would open her card and show me. "Look, Craig! Grandma gave me twenty dollars! Did you get a check too?"

I'd open my card and peek, and I'd say, "A hundred dollars! Are you kidding me? She gave me a hundred dollars!"

Lisa would be crestfallen. She'd ask, "Really?"

I'd fold my check, stick it in my pocket, say "Yeah," and just casually walk away, whistling or something. Sometimes Lisa would get so upset, she'd cry. I don't know why it felt so good to make her feel so bad. (I'm not proud of this now, of course.)

And then, inevitably, Grandma found out.

The next Christmas, when I opened up my twenty-dollar check and said, "A hundred dollars!" Lisa opened up her hundred-dollar check and said, "A hundred dollars!" My grandma taught me to rejoice with those who really *do* get a hundred-dollar gift.

When someone else gets something you were hoping for, you should rejoice with them. I think one of the best examples of this in Scripture is between Saul's son Jonathan and his friend David. Remember earlier I talked about King Saul envying David. Well, that same King Saul had a son, Jonathan. David and Jonathan were best friends. By all earthly rights, Jonathan should've been the heir to his father's throne. For most of Jonathan's youth, he probably fully expected, maybe even dreamed about, how one day he would become king. Of course, if you know the story, God had other plans. Saul sinned, and God chose David to replace Saul as Israel's king.

Most of us, if we were in Jonathan's position, would be angry. Not Jonathan. Even when Saul was crazy with jealous rage, hunting David down to kill him, Jonathan took David's side. In fact, look what Jonathan said to David in 1 Samuel 23:17: "Don't be afraid … My father Saul will not lay a hand on you. You will be king over Israel, and I will be second to you." He was telling David, "I'll serve you. I've got your back. I rejoice with you in your success. You've got what really was mine, and what I wanted, but God had something else planned. More power to you, man. I celebrate with you."

Similar things happen to all of us. You want that promotion at work. Someone else gets it. What should your response be? "Congratulations!" If there was something you were hoping to get, but someone else got it instead: "Way to go." Have you ever prayed for something that you desperately wanted, and you were just waiting and waiting for God to deliver? And then you saw God answer someone else on that same kind of prayer? "Awesome. Way to go!" Rejoice with those who rejoice. Instead of resenting their blessings, celebrate them.

Be Careful Where You Step

Ecclesiastes 6:9 says, "Better what the eye sees than the roving of the appetite. This too is meaningless, a chasing after the wind." God has put blessings right in front of us. It's easy to let our appetites rove. But when you let your eyes wander, looking for something else, you might as well be chasing after wind. It's better to enjoy what God has given you than to look around to see whose grass is greener. It's easy to always look for more. Unless you have one of everything on the planet, then there's always somebody who has something you don't. Theirs may be newer. Theirs may be bigger. Theirs may be shinier. But if you notice that, it means you're making comparisons. (And we've already talked about that.) What about what God has already given you? Are you grateful for the things you do have?

Don't misunderstand. I'm not saying that someone else's grass isn't actually greener than yours. It may be. But there's an important principle at work here: their grass may be greener than yours, but from where you're standing, you may not be able to see all the poop in their yard. People have said to me before, "Craig, I wish I had your life." I can understand that. No question about it, I have a great life. But I have to tell you, a lot of hard things go on behind the scenes. There's a lot of poop in my yard, and not just figuratively. I have six kids. I've changed more dirty diapers in my day than any three ordinary families. Hard times are everywhere.

If the grass is greener in someone else's yard, maybe it's time you watered your own. How long has it been since you've taken stock of what God's given you and said, "Father, thank you"?

I used to have a really bad habit that I now believe was insulting to God. In fact, just being honest, I still have to work not to do it. I would qualify my thankfulness with a big "but." If someone said, "I really like your house," then I said something like, "Yeah, it's great, we really love it, *but* we really need to redo the kitchen." Or if someone told me how much they appreciated me as their pastor, I said, "I feel humbled, honored, and privileged that I get to serve God's kingdom as my job, *but* I sure wish I didn't have to work weekends." You know, sort of in that joking way that we try to disguise the truth.

Then God's Spirit really began to convict me: I needed to get rid of my big buts. "I'm thankful for the house that God has provided for us." Period. "I'm thankful for what I get to do." Period. I heartily encourage you to do the same; get rid of your big buts. Be thankful. No more buts. Embrace God's goodness to you: "Rejoice always, pray continually, give thanks in all circumstances; for this is God's will for you in Christ Jesus" (1 Thess. 5:16 – 18). If you're in Christ Jesus, there's your answer. Be thankful. Be satisfied. Be content in all circumstances.

Your Heart's Desire

One way to appreciate all that we have is to spend time with people who are truly grateful for and joyful about all that they have. If they have less than we do, it can be very humbling. When I first became a pastor, there was a six-year-old girl in our church who was dying. We prayed and prayed for her, but she just continued to get worse.

Near the end, I went to visit this precious little girl in the hospital. Her treatments had taken her hair, her color, and the last of her strength. I did the pastor thing, making small talk with her and her parents, trying to smile a lot and lift their spirits, and praying with them. But I felt so helpless. Finally I said, "Sweetheart, what do you want? Anything. You name it. If there's anything at all I can do for you or get for you, please just name it, and it's yours."

For a moment, she just locked eyes with me and didn't say anything, like she was deep in thought. As I waited for her answer, I couldn't help thinking of all the things she might have been dreaming about in the past weeks: Playing with other kids? Going to see a movie with her friends? Going home? Just taking a walk outside?

This tiny six-year-old girl drew in a deep breath and sighed. Then she said, "Well, I've got my mommy and daddy here. I've got my two favorite sticker books. I've got my dolly, and I've got Jesus in my heart. What else could a little kid want?"

Just a few weeks later, I did that little girl's funeral. But that moment at the hospital will resonate with me for as long as I live. I don't know how your story goes, but here's mine: I get to serve the greatest God, the creator and builder of the universe, and I get to do it full-time. I get to love and share his truth with the greatest people, and that is my calling. I've got my best friend, who also happens to be my wife, who has sacrificed so much of herself to give me six kids. I've got the greatest friends that a guy could ever ask for. I've got the best staff working in God's kingdom today. And of course, I've got Jesus Christ, the Living Son of the almighty God, dwelling inside me. What more could any guy ever want?

I hope that you can celebrate God's goodness in the lives of others, that you can embrace God's goodness to you, and that you never envy again.

Jesus is truly enough for our heart's desire.

7

Rage Rash

Neutralizing the Acid of Anger

Anger is an acid that can do more harm to the vessel
in which it is stored than to anything on which it is poured.
—Mark Twain

Amy and I don't go out to the movies very often, so when we do, we really want to enjoy the experience. In addition to spending the time alone with my wife, I want to make sure we're getting our money's worth. But so many other people seem determined to ruin our date at the movies.

Amy and I always make a point to go early enough so we can get the best seats, half-way back from the screen and middle of the row. Everybody knows the middle is the best place to sit to watch a movie. In the front, you're looking up at some actor's twelve-foot-high nostrils.

Too far left or right and it's like trying to watch a movie in the side mirrors of your car.

We sit down, the entire row vacant on both sides of us, and then inevitably a "space invader" arrives. You've probably experienced one too. The late arriver walks straight into your row, then plops down directly next to you, clearly breaking the empty-seat rule: "If plenty of seats are available, leave a vacant seat between you and the person next to you." If you are a guy, there is nothing worse than another guy sitting right by you. The entire time, you're battling over that disputed armrest border territory. Which means sometimes, there's going to be guy skin against guy skin. *So* wrong.

Then there's the "switchboard operator," who thinks that watching a movie presents the ideal opportunity to catch up on a few phone calls and texts. Their phone rings — and they actually answer! Believe it or not, I've even seen people *make* a phone call while they're sitting in a movie. I didn't pay twenty bucks so that my wife and I could listen to someone tell their mom the results of their cat's lab work.

Then there's the "commentator." Like a play-by-play analyst at a football game, this person provides running comments (and questions!) throughout the entire film. They never shut up. Some commentators are clueless from the beginning and never catch on. "Now, who's this guy? What kind of car is that? What did she say?" And if they're not asking questions that the rest of us know the answer to, then they're pointing out the obvious. "So that's where the money went! Yes, I knew she was trouble when she walked in. You could tell that he wasn't really a crook."

Just as bad, there's what I call the "spoiler," who has the superpower of being able to see five minutes into the future. Worse, they believe it's their responsibility to make sure everybody knows that *they* know exactly what's going to happen next. "Ooooh, he did it. That's your guy, right there. I'll bet he's on the roof with a helicopter. Yup, told you. She's gonna steal that briefcase, just watch."

You're welcome to laugh at me for letting such little, petty things bother me so much. It might even irritate you that I make a big deal out of such small stuff. But how about you: what are your pet peeves? What are some of those little habits of other people that make you want to push them down the escalator at the mall? Now here's an even bigger question: how do you deal with your anger on a daily basis? Or do you deal with it at all?

Smoldering Inferno

So many little things can get under our skin. Someone cuts in front of you in traffic. Someone's rude to you, or speaks rudely to a person you care about. Someone you talked to today said something really arrogant — like they think they have all the answers. Your boss takes credit for your best work, and then unfairly hangs blame on you for a project that he caused to be late. It could be the other members of your work team don't do their jobs. Your husband leaves his underwear on the floor. Your wife squeezes the toothpaste from the middle, mangling the entire tube in the process. Little things can irritate us.

And there's more than enough big things to make our blood pressure skyrocket. Natural disasters claim thousands of lives. Poverty runs rampant in many parts of the world. Children go to sleep at night with empty bellies, while people only a few miles away throw away pounds and pounds of uneaten food from overpriced buffets. Girls and boys suffer abuse from teachers, coaches, and even family members. Innocent bystanders are shot and killed in the crossfire of drug wars. Corporations exploit the earth's resources for billions of dollars and excrete toxic waste into the land and seas. People are tricked, kidnapped, taken advantage of — even sold as slaves. With all of our advancements in technology that shrink our world into a global community, we're still battling human traffickers in the twenty-first century! And I'm barely scratching the surface of the travesties of justice in our world today.

Do these issues upset you, keep you awake some nights, force you to change the channel or leave the room? What really makes your blood boil? What are the things that eat at you, stressing you out, robbing you of peace and joy in life? Where does this anger even come from? And maybe more importantly, what are we supposed to do about it?

The Bible has a few things to say about anger. In fifteen different instances, the Bible mentions both the word *anger* and the word *fire* in the same verse. The comparison is not only dramatic and colorful but very revealing about the qualities of this volatile emotion. Fire is a gift that can sustain life. When it's contained, when you control it, when you manage it, fire can warm you. You can cook with it. You can use it to heat water for a warm bath, or use it to light candles or lamps to illuminate dark nights.

However, when a fire rages out of control, it can destroy everything in its path, consuming in just a few moments everything that we've spent a lifetime building. Wildfires can destroy thousands of acres of timber, wildlife, and natural resources. Fire can even claim lives. According to recent data from the Centers for Disease Control and Prevention, fire-related deaths in the US average nearly three thousand each year.

Just like fire, our anger can be used constructively or destructively. Used as a catalyst for justice and the pursuit of God's righteousness, anger can cleanse, restore, and unite. Or, if we allow our anger to rage out of control in conjunction with our desires, frustrations, and grievances, it can lead us to hurt others and ourselves. Our anger can reflect God's character or it can distance us from him. It can invite God's Spirit into our lives to examine a hard truth, or it can become an open invitation to an unwanted houseguest.

Your Unwelcome Houseguest

When was the last time you invited the devil into your heart for a sleepover? Strange question? Not if you consider Ephesians 4:26 – 27: " 'In your anger do not sin': Do not let the sun go down while you are still angry, and do not give the devil a foothold." The opening admonition — "In your anger do not sin" — comes from Psalm 4:4. It's important to note that this verse tells us that anger in and of itself is not sinful.

Again, just like fire, there are two types of anger. The first, the "good" kind, is what we might call sanctified or righteous anger. It's the powerful emotion we experience when we get upset at something that affronts God, something opposing his truth. This kind of anger leads us to a righteous reaction. We take a stand, speak the truth, and express the problem in a way that accurately represents God's heart.

The "bad" kind of anger, on the other hand, usually results when we lose control of our emotions and take matters into our own hands. Sinful anger is getting angry at something — maybe even something legitimate, something that also angers God — but then allowing that anger to lead us to do the wrong thing.

The second part of that Ephesians verse says, "Do not let the sun go down while you are still angry." If you're angry, you should deal with it. Why? Because the Bible tells us what happens if we *do* go to bed angry: we give the devil a foothold. The Greek word for foothold is *topos*, which literally means "opportunity" or "location." It's an occupied territory. If you open the door to the devil through your anger, you're offering him a guest room inside your heart. Talk about sleeping with the enemy!

And yet, Scripture is full of examples of people who allowed the enemy to set up camp in their hearts. In prior chapters, we've already looked at the first recorded sibling rivalry between Adam and Eve's sons, Cain and Abel. Both made offerings to God. God accepted Abel's sacrifice because he made it exactly as God had instructed. But God didn't accept Cain's because Cain decided to do it his own way. When God rejected what Cain brought, Cain became extremely angry. He opened the door and allowed the devil to walk right in. Consider what God said to Cain: "Why are you angry? Why is your face downcast? If you do what is right, will you not be accepted? But if you do not do what is right, sin is crouching at your door; it desires to have you, but you must rule over it" (Gen. 4:6 – 7).

You know the rest of the story. Cain let his anger overtake him, and he murdered his brother, Abel. God warned Cain that sin was crouching at his door. But instead of locking the door of his heart and then barricading it, Cain opened it wide and allowed enemy occupation. By allowing his anger to rule over him, his lack of containment led straight to sin. And not just any sin, but taking a human life.

Hopefully you've never allowed your anger to reach the boiling point of taking someone's life. However, if you've allowed your anger free reign enough even to wish that someone else were dead, then in God's eyes, you're just as guilty as Cain. In his Sermon on the Mount, Jesus explained, "You have heard that it was said to the people long ago, 'You shall not murder, and anyone who murders will be subject to judgment.' But I tell you that anyone who is angry with a brother or sister will be subject to judgment. Again, anyone who says to a brother or sister, 'Raca,' is answerable to the court. And anyone who says, 'You fool!' will be in danger of the fire of hell" (Matt. 5:21 – 22).

When I think about how easily I'm angered, my heart sinks. Jesus said that we don't have to murder someone to be guilty of killing them with our thoughts. He says that if we even call them "fool," we're endangering our souls. *Raca* was an Aramaic term of contempt, not unlike the way we use "idiot" or "jerk." If I'm honest, I know that the terms I've thought of, and even said, when mad at someone are far worse. Yes, God's Word is very clear that if we don't get a handle on our anger, it will get a handle on us.

Anger Management

How does your anger usually manifest? What's your default style of conflict management? Most of us express our anger in one of two ways, either with a hair-trigger or a slow cooker. "Spewers" have no problem openly expressing their anger. A spewer has a short fuse and a hot temper. If you're a spewer, when you get angry, everyone around you knows it. Maybe you rationalize it. Like sometimes things just build up inside, and you need to open that release valve and let off some steam.

Consider what the Bible says about this approach to dealing with anger in Proverbs 14:17: "A quick-tempered person does foolish things." Proverbs 29:11 says the same thing another way: "Fools give full vent to their rage." So, just to be clear, if you vent your anger, the Bible says you're a fool. Fortunately, the second half of verse 11 tells us the alternative: "the wise bring calm in the end."

Years ago, I had a reputation for being a bit quick on the temper trigger. And truth be told, I earned that badge. Once, I went out to lunch with a group of pastors from our staff and several of their wives. We had been having a great time together, when one of the pastors, Sam, who's a good friend of mine, had to leave early for an afternoon meeting. His wife, Jayme, stayed with the rest of us while we finished lunch. Afterward, as we were all walking out of the restaurant together, a pick-up truck drove by with three guys in it and the windows rolled down. As they passed by us in the parking lot, they shouted some obscene comments to Jayme.

Since Sam wasn't there to defend his wife, and because he's my good friend, I did what I had to do, the only sensible thing I could do, what any of you would have done — I pursued them on foot in a blind rage. It's true. Fortunately, the other pastors who were with me were older, wiser, and more mature than I was. Jerry, who's a few years older, ran after me. (I didn't know if he was planning to try to stop me or to back me up.) But Kevin, who is older than either Jerry or me, was the wisest of all. He ran in the opposite direction — straight to our church van. He jumped in, got it started, picked up the ladies, and came after us.

By this time, I had flagged down the guys in the truck and gotten them to stop. I positioned myself menacingly next to the driver's open window, looked them all over to make sure they didn't go to our church, and then lit into them with a verbal tongue lashing. Jerry caught up with me on foot just as Kevin arrived with the van. In a flawlessly executed maneuver, Kevin eased up alongside us, Jerry grabbed me and hauled me in through the open van door, and we made our escape, all in one fluid motion that would've made Jason Bourne proud.

If you can relate to my explosion, if you look around and see substantial collateral damage in the wake of your rage, then you're a spewer like me. Or as the Bible calls us — fools.

Slow Burn

You're not off the hook, though, if you're congratulating yourself because you're not a spewer. The other way many people deal with their anger is to just bottle it up; I call them "stewers." You might not explode and lash out, but your anger is still there. Instead of an exploding volcano, you're more like a wildfire hiding below the tree-line after a lightning strike. The sparks of your anger come out by rolling your eyes or being sarcastic. You hold a grudge and look for the opportunity for payback. Maybe you're hypercritical and judgmental as a result of your slow-burning coals of anger.

David, in the Old Testament, was a frequent stewer. Psalm 32:3 records a time when David was really upset and holding it in: "When I kept silent, my bones wasted away through my groaning all day long." David bottled it up, like so many of us do. We get upset, and rather than talking things out in a healthy way, we pour them in our internal crock pot and pressure cook them.

Sure, on the outside, you might look like you have yourself under control, but just below the surface, you're smoldering, building up heat that could erupt into flames at any minute. What stewers practice is the opposite of love. First Corinthians 13:5 says that love "is not easily angered, it keeps no record of wrongs." But stewers keep a long list of offenses: "She did this ... He did that ... I'll never forgive them for ..." They stew and stew and stew on the ways they feel others have wronged them. Whether served hot or cold, anger stew is a poisonous dish, a carcinogen that will grow a cancer inside you.

In the story of the prodigal son, you may remember the younger brother said, "Dad, give me all my stuff." (I'm paraphrasing — see Luke 15:12.) His father gave him his inheritance, and he left and partied hard, blowing through his cash faster than a first-timer in Vegas. When he finally came home, empty-handed and ashamed, everyone was shocked when his father loved him openly and took him back in.

And not only did he take him back, he actually threw a huge party for him. When the older brother found out what was going on, however, he got so angry, he wouldn't even go in the house. Stewing and storming around outside, the older brother finally let it out when his father came out to talk to him: "I kept all your stupid rules. I've worked like a dog for you and always did everything you asked. You never gave me a party! It's just not fair!" (Again, my paraphrase; see Luke 15:29 – 30.) No doubt, the older brother was a classic stewer.

Fire Extinguisher

Regardless of whether we're a spewer or a stewer, we're likely going to wind up in the sewer unless we learn to control our response to our anger and express it productively. If you know that your anger is leading you to sin, either inside your heart or with external behavior, then you must put a fire extinguisher to good use. Ask God to quench that fire with his Spirit. Proverbs 17:14 says, "Starting a quarrel is like breaching a dam; so drop the matter before a dispute breaks out." Put your fire out before that dam breaks and carries you both away. Drop it. Let it go.

While putting out the fire might feel impossible, it's a choice. You can control it. Before you start telling me that having a quick temper is just part of who you are, consider this. Have you ever seen someone (or even been this person) who's blowing up, letting it rip, when the phone rings. The person answers, "Hello? Oh, hey, how's it going? Yeah, things are fine. Wow — that's great. Praise God. Sure. I've been praying for you. Okay. Let's get together. We'll do that. You bet. Blessings.

Bye." Then they hang up and go, "Now, where was I? Oh, yeah …" and then resume their screaming rant right where they left off. As funny as it may be, it's clear evidence that we can control our anger by making the right choices.

I challenge you to start practicing this kind of self-control today. Maybe you're waiting. The person you're waiting for is late — again. Drop it. Nobody's going to die if they're late. Or maybe somebody loaded the dishwasher wrong. Instead of fuming, let it go. Praise God that at least they tried. Perhaps there's one co-worker who keeps getting under your skin. Stop and consider that God loves that person just as much as God loves you.

Some things (a lot of things, as it turns out) are just not worth getting angry about. James 1:19 – 20 says, "My dear brothers and sisters, take note of this: Everyone should be quick to listen, slow to speak and slow to become angry, because human anger does not produce the righteousness that God desires." So there are basically three things we can do. In order:

1. Listen.
2. Take some time to process before speaking.
3. Don't jump straight to being angry.

It's taken years for me to become slow to anger. I attribute it to two things. First, I've consistently submitted myself to the truth that my anger won't fulfill what God desires — his righteousness. I want to be the man that God desires me to be. Completely. Second, God has honored that commitment. He's in the process of making me more like himself. Seven different books of the Bible all mention the same character attribute of God. Do you know what it is? Seven different writers all noticed that God is "slow to anger" and "abounding in love."

With his help, I'm becoming slow to anger and abounding in love. And I'm not the only one who thinks so. A long time ago, we were looking for an assistant for me. One of the challenges in filling this position is that many people see me through rose-colored glasses as "Pastor Craig," the great guy who's always godly, joyful, compassionate, and loving. Consequently, applicants had a hard time thinking of me as "regular Craig," their boss who has good days and bad days like everyone else.

So our entire executive team interviewed each finalist. When we were meeting with Sarah, the woman we ultimately chose, one of my colleagues asked her, "Do you think you could handle Craig if he got angry?"

Well, I was immediately offended. "I don't get angry," I said.

Another team member said, "Yeah, you do," while the others snickered.

And I said, "Whatever! We deal with intense things here sometimes, but it's not that big of a deal."

Sarah squinted at me. "Yeah, I understand. No problem."

Another staff member looked at the ceiling and asked, "What if Craig, oh, I don't know, say ... threw a pencil?"

"Wait a minute! That happened only one time! Once! Are you ever gonna let me live that down?"

As their questions continued down the same path, I could feel my temperature rising.

I kept interrupting, "I don't get that mad!"

They all smiled and nodded at me. "Yes, you do."

"No, I don't!" I couldn't help raising my voice a little.

One of them looked at Sarah and said, "See?"

"This isn't really fair," I said as meekly as I could.

After Sarah had worked with me for several years, I was preparing a message about anger. We were talking through some of the points in my outline when she stopped and said, "You know, Craig, I can't remember the last time I've seen you angry. It's been years."

This was the greatest compliment she could've given me! Reining in your anger — and changing your reputation — is possible. If your anger is poisoning your life, ask God for patience and wisdom to help you. If it's sinful anger, ask God to put it out. Stop making excuses. He wants to make you more like himself.

Fired Up

The other kind of anger, what I call sanctified anger, requires a different response. Scripture offers several examples of Jesus getting angry — but he never sinned. His was a righteous anger. One of my favorites is a story in Mark 3:1 – 6 about a man with a shriveled hand. This man happened to be in the synagogue on the Sabbath. The Pharisees were there, too, watching Jesus to see if he might dare to heal someone on the Sabbath.

Apparently, they considered performing a miracle on their holy day to be a monumental sin. Jesus seemed to know what they were thinking. In verse 4, he asked them, "Which is lawful on the Sabbath: to do good or to do evil, to save life or to kill?" But they refused to answer. Verse 5 says, "He looked around at them *in anger … deeply distressed* at their stubborn hearts" (emphasis mine). Jesus was mad. He was angry. All he wanted to do was demonstrate God's love to people in need. But his detractors were watching his every move, hell-bent on keeping God's freedom out of their temple.

If I had Jesus' power, I don't know if I could have been so kind. I might raise my hands, and *bam!* they'd all have hemorrhoids. Okay, so maybe that's just me. And that would be letting my anger lead me to sin. Instead, Jesus "said to the man, 'Stretch out your hand.' He stretched it out, and his hand was completely restored" (Mark 3:5). Rather than allowing his anger to cause him to sin, Jesus redirected his anger to do something righteous.

It's okay to be angry. You can be angry and not sin. Let the Spirit of God fan that flame. Is your marriage struggling? Get angry. Not at your spouse — get mad at the evil one who's moved his stuff into your home. Put him on notice. Kick him out. Are you sick of seeing disease and poverty and cruelty, maybe in another country, maybe even in your own city? Fan that flame. Pour some gasoline on it. Get angry. Do something righteous about it.

Do you love someone who's wallowing in self destruction, making one bad decision after another? Get angry. Reach out to them with everything in you. Do you struggle with sinful anger? Get mad at it! Attack it with righteous rage. Turn its power into a righteous anger that begins to fulfill God's will for your life. Get angry about the things that anger God.

Who's in charge in your life? Sin is crouching at your door. Don't let your hair-trigger anger tell you what to do anymore. Be wise. Don't give your enemy even a spot of ground to stand on, not a nanometer. Don't spew like a volcano. Chasing down cars in parking lots won't accomplish the righteousness that God desires. Don't stew on it. Love keeps no record of wrongs.

Instead, spend quiet, slow time with God, in prayer and in his Word, and learn what things make him angry. Then, when you feel your pulse starting to race, your temperature starting to rise, the veins in your neck starting to pop out, ask yourself, Where is this heading? If it's toward sin, put it out. Drop it. But if it's toward righteousness, fan the flame. Invite God to make you more like himself — and then let him.

8

Scare Pollution

Unlocking the Chokehold of Fear

I have never known more than fifteen minutes of anxiety
or fear. When I feel fearful emotions overtaking me,
I just close my eyes and thank God that He is still on
the throne, reigning over everything, and I take comfort
in His control over the affairs of my life.
—John Wesley

When my younger sister, Lisa, was little, she had the most irrational fear. Before she went to bed each night, she had to make sure her closet door was completely closed. I mean shut tight, with maybe even a chair and a few toys in front of it. If her closet door was slightly open, even half an inch, she believed that whatever was in there (her clothes? a hundred hair ribbons? her Barbie dolls?) could slip out and grab her. For whatever reason, she was convinced that as long as that closet door was closed, she'd be safe.

Of course, when I was a kid, I never had any silly fears like that — mine were all perfectly reasonable. For example, I knew that once you get in bed, you should never leave a hand or foot dangling over the edge. There's no surer way to be dragged away by whatever evil creatures hide underneath your bed at night! And of course the only way to keep them from grabbing you when you're getting into bed is to get a running start and leap over them. Then there's that inevitable trip to the bathroom in the middle of the night, when you have to stand up and get a good jump off your mattress to be sure you clear them.

What were you afraid of as a child? The dark? Thunderstorms? Crossing bridges? Spiders? (I know a lot of people who are still afraid of spiders even as adults.) Shower curtains? To this day, I still can't stand to see a closed shower curtain; even Martha Stewart says they need to be pulled to the side (she says left, I say right) with clear and complete visibility into the shower stall or tub. What? You never saw *Psycho*? Or about a dozen other scary movies? Everyone knows that the crazy killer/zombie/vampire/ax murderer/creepy kidnapper always hides in the shower.

The Not-So-Fantastic Four

We often look back and laugh at our childhood fears, but most of us continue to battle a variety of very adult fears each day: losing our job, getting sick, running out of money, going bankrupt, getting a divorce, being betrayed by those we love. The more fear we allow into our lives, the more we struggle to grow spiritually. It's like trying to plant an apple orchard in downtown L.A. The smog and air pollution is going to rob the saplings of the precious oxygen they need and contaminate their water supply. Fear poisons us a little each day if we don't face it head-on and nullify its power.

Interestingly enough, when human babies are born, we have only two natural fears: the fear of falling and the fear of loud noises. This means that all those other things we're afraid of are learned fears, fears we've accumulated, mostly through experience. Like a pack on our back that accumulates into a burden the size of a dumpster, our fears weigh us down and prevent us from traveling through life with speed and grace. Generally, most of our adult fears fall into four categories.

1. Fear of Loss

One of our basic human fears, the fear of loss can take many forms. If you're married, thoughts of losing your spouse may prey on your peace of mind. Almost every parent I know has at some point dealt with the fear of losing a child, or at least the fear of something bad happening to one of their children.

Of course, some people fear financial loss, whether from a lost job or a failed investment. Others fear losing control — that if they can't keep tabs on everything (and everyone) and keep all their plates spinning just the way they want, their world will collapse around them.

What is it for you? What have you feared losing before? What are you most afraid of losing right now?

2. Fear of Failure

Another common fear is the fear of failure. To be honest, thoughts of failure probably plague me the most. Sometimes I find myself worrying that I'm not up to the demands of a goal that's set before me. I'm afraid that I just won't have what it takes to see it through.

A lot of people would like to tackle some challenge, especially a new venture they've always dreamed about, but they're afraid they might not be successful (or at least what they consider to be successful). Maybe you've wanted to start your own business, but then you thought, "I don't know what I'm doing — this will be like throwing money down the drain." Maybe you've felt a burden to start a ministry in an area in which you're really passionate. But you can't help thinking, "I just don't think I'm good enough to do it." Fear of failure can paralyze us from starting any new endeavor: launching a business, going back to school, pursuing a relationship, or even just reaching out to someone with a phone call. You're not sure if you'll be able to do it, so you never even try. That's the power of the toxic fear of failure.

What are you afraid of failing at?

3. Fear of Rejection

Many of us fear rejection and abandonment. I've known perfectly decent guys who wanted to ask out a woman but hesitated because they thought, "Now why would a girl like that ever want to go out with a guy like me?" I've known married people who lived in constant fear that their spouse was going to just up and leave them.

Other people are absolutely controlled by a people-pleasing mindset that's anchored in a fear of rejection. They want everybody to accept them, so they wonder, "Will she like this hairstyle? What will he think if I don't agree to this deal? I better go or they won't like me. I don't want to upset anyone if I don't have to."

Are you ever afraid that people might not like you as you are?

4. Fear of the Unknown

Finally, most of us dread not knowing what lies ahead. Many people can't help wondering things like, "What if I get sick with some serious illness? Or what if that happens to someone I love?" They worry about things they can't control: "What if I lose my job? What's going to happen in the future? What if no one ever truly loves me?"

What are you afraid of knowing? What would you prefer to stay in the dark about?

(((

When you feel fearful, you need to acknowledge this truth: our all-knowing, always-present, all-powerful Father doesn't give us fear. "For God has not given us a spirit of fear, but of power and of love and of a sound mind" (2 Tim. 1:7 NKJV). Why then do so many of us find ourselves consumed with fear, when it's clear that what God has given us is power, love, and a sound mind?

If you're always worried, always anxious, always overwhelmed, living paralyzed, then you need to realize this important truth. Fear comes from our enemy. He lobs smoke bombs at us constantly, each time hoping that we'll mistake it for a live grenade. If your life is polluted by fear, it's time to clear the smoke and take a breath of fresh air.

Imaginations Gone Wild

People often say that fear is the opposite of faith, but I respectfully disagree. The way I see it, fear actually relies on faith — it's simply *faith in the wrong things*. Fear is placing your faith in "what-ifs" rather than in "God is." It's allowing your imagination to wander down a long dark alley of possibilities and get mugged every couple of steps. Almost everyone who allows themselves to be taken hostage by what-ifs discovers that the only thing binding them is their own imagination.

You know who really wrestled with this? Moses. In the Old Testament, when God first appeared to Moses, calling on him to deliver the Hebrew people out of slavery to the Egyptians, he chose to do so by talking from a burning bush. Now, that would probably get most people's attention. And yet, following this encounter, we see Moses immediately start playing the what-if game with God.

In Exodus 3, God reveals to Moses his entire plan and Moses' role in it, even assuring Moses that God himself will be with him. Then, in the very next chapter, in Exodus 4:1, Moses responds by answering God, "What if they do not believe me or listen to me and say, 'The LORD did not appear to you'?" This is the same game most of us play, especially when God calls us because he wants to use our lives to do something significant.

Rather than considering that God knows what he's doing and trusting him, we immediately roll out a long list of what-ifs. "Sounds good, Lord, but what if I can't do it? What if the economy drops? What if I lose my job? What if I get sick? What if my spouse cheats on me? What if my kids get hurt? What if we get in a car accident? What if I never get married? What if I do get married, but it's to a jerk? What if we can't have kids? What if we have too many kids? What if our cat gets pregnant ... again?" There are just so many bad things that could happen in life. It seems like we spend a huge amount of time brainstorming a list of everything that could go wrong, instead of better using that same energy to ask God for steps we could take that will help us meaningfully get in on what he's doing.

Your what-ifs do matter, though. In fact, if you stop and analyze them, you can usually gain some vital insight. The first is that *what you fear reveals what you value the most.* Examining what you fear can illuminate your priorities, which are always good to know. For example, if you fear losing your marriage, that shows that you really value your commitment to your marriage. If you fear that something bad may happen to your children, that shows that you really value your kids. If you fear losing your job or losing your money, you value financial security and stability. While none of these are inherently bad things to place value on, focusing negatively on any of them can lead you down a poison path to worry rather than leading you to positive action.

When you have persistent fear in a given area of your life, it can be an indicator that you're not depending on God to handle it. In other words, *what you fear reveals where you trust God the least.* And this usually means that you're not asking him for direction in that area, either. Let's say that you're constantly worried about your marriage. Have you asked God to make your marriage better — and then trusted him to actually do it? If you pray, but then you keep worrying about it, your actions are communicating, "Sure, I prayed, but that's not enough. I don't need God to intervene on this one as much as he needs me to."

Or if you worry that something bad might happen to your children, you're essentially telling God, "I don't really believe you're good enough. I don't believe that your plan and your purposes will come through for my children. So for my part, I'm going to contribute by worrying." If you're constantly worrying about financial stability, then your actions are saying, "God, I don't really trust you to provide for me."

In fact, in Matthew 6:27, Jesus makes it clear how much good all our angst does us: "Can any one of you by worrying add a single hour to your life?" Obviously, the answer is no. So why do we do it? Because we're afraid to trust God with every area and every hour of our lives. Because anticipating the worst allows us to believe we have some semblance of control; we won't be surprised when something terrible happens because we've already imagined it and prepared ourselves.

So how do we find our way out? I believe we have to face our greatest fears in order to reach our greatest potential. And the only way to do this is to allow God to lead you.

Gone for Good

My wife and I experienced this firsthand. A little more than ten years ago, Amy was popping out kids like a short order cook flips out pancakes during the morning rush. It seemed like she was constantly having babies. We'd just look at each other and get pregnant! While we were grateful for each new addition to our family, each took its toll. All those kids in that short span of time, one after another, proved to be really hard on her body. Soon Amy began facing some troubling, significant health issues on an ongoing basis.

Amy began experiencing numbness on one side of her body more and more frequently. She was nauseated a lot, in near-constant pain, and weak pretty much all the time. We visited doctor after doctor ... after doctor ... after doctor ... after doctor. Even after what seemed like hundreds of tests, no one was able to diagnose her condition. Even worse, no one could offer us any suggestions for treatment to improve it. Her condition was compounded even further by the fear it was causing both of us.

For months, each night we'd cry out to God together before we went to bed. Her condition continued to worsen, and some nights Amy honestly didn't believe she'd wake up the next morning. Her body wracked with pain, my wife would tell me that she loved me and go over what she wanted me to do for the kids if we lost her sometime during the night. It was that intense. Convinced she was dying, with hope waning because no doctor could tell us what was going on, she and I spent those nights in constant fear. Each day that she woke up was like a gift to us, one more day with her family, one more day to hope for relief.

With nowhere else to turn, Amy kept turning to God. She continued seeking him through his Word. She had her Bible open all the time, studying it as if her very life depended on it. She prayed without ceasing. She cried out to God, telling him what she was afraid of and asking him for answers. She asked him to show her what she could do — what she *should* do. She prayed the words she found in the Scriptures. She organized a kind of prayer barter system, where she'd tell people things she needed prayer for, and she'd pray for their needs. She would ask certain people that God laid on her heart to pray for very specific, focused things for her. Every waking moment, Amy was following hard after God, searching and looking for him wherever he could be found. She was diligent, purposeful, and relentless.

Then, in the middle of her spiritual pursuit, God showed her something that changed everything. One simple verse grabbed her attention and never let go. Hebrews 11:6 says, "Without faith it is impossible to please God." In an instant, Amy realized that she'd been living by fear and not by faith. And her faithless heart couldn't please God. Amy decided to put all her faith and trust into her God. Like someone flipping a light switch from off to on, Amy switched from fear of the worst case scenario to faith in God's best promises.

That's when God did what only he could do. God delivered her from her worst fear. It evaporated, just disappeared, gone. Virtually at the same time, her health began to improve. Each day, she got stronger and had more energy, with fewer aches and pains than the day before. After a few weeks, she was back at a hundred percent, and perhaps even healthier than before.

To this day, the only explanation we have is that God delivered Amy from her sickness. And by the time our ordeal was over, she had formed stronger habits centered around the pursuit of God in every corner of her life. She has maintained that lifestyle of pursuing him constantly. To the same extent that Amy had been consumed by fear before, now she is so consumed with faithfulness that it positively overflows out of her. She is truly fearless.

Name Calling

For Amy, the turning point was when she uncovered what she was most afraid of happening. When Amy faced her greatest fear, it revealed what she valued the most: she wanted to be here with and for her family. It was also obvious to her where she trusted God the least: she was convinced that she was simply going to die — that her health would not return and that our six children and I would be left to raise ourselves without her. She was afraid of an uncertain future, afraid that her mystery illness would take her life. So that's what she took to God. That's what she asked him to deliver her from, and that's what she entrusted him to handle. She didn't just quit. She didn't just resign herself to being a host for the parasite of fear. Instead she connected herself to God as intimately as she could.

If you're struggling to trust God in some area of your life, I believe you must first identify what you're afraid of. You can't know where to start to address it if you're still pretending it doesn't exist. So admit it. Identify it clearly. Until you do, it will continue to be that elephant in the room, that huge dark cloud hovering over you that you're not willing to talk about. So do some name calling. Check the label and see the brand of fear you're wearing.

Once you identify it, then you can surrender it to God. You can commit to trust him to give you the power to overcome your fear once and for all. Let me clarify this. I'm *not* saying to just "give it over to God," and then pretend like it's not a problem anymore. No, what I'm saying is that you must allow God to give you strength, wisdom, and courage in defeating your fear once and for all.

The Bible says in James, "If any of you lacks wisdom, you should ask God, who gives generously to all without finding fault, and it will be given to you" (1:5). Ask God to show you whatever you can do within your power to minimize the risk of that fear becoming real- ized. Then, whatever God reveals to you, do that. Beyond that, choose with every bit of faith you have to trust that God will be faithful, like his Word says he will be. He will be faithful to see you through, and he will always provide a way for you to endure.

In the Old Testament, David grew up as a simple shepherd boy before becoming king of Israel. God first prepared him, then led him to do some amazing things, like killing the giant Goliath. And even after God had made it clear that he was to be the future king over Israel, sending his prophet Samuel to anoint David (see 1 Samuel 16), a symbolic act marking him as God's chosen, he faced many obstacles and waited many years before assuming the throne. Not the least of those obstacles was the reigning king, Saul, who felt very threatened by this up-and-comer. In fact, Saul's anxiety became so great that he began to loathe the dynamic young warrior-poet. Finally, his fear-based hatred reached the boiling point, and King Saul issued an order to his son and to his men, "I want you to go hunt David down ... and kill him" (see 1 Samuel 19).

Now, it's easy to look at this situation and think, "Wow, how terrible. It must've been really hard for David to have the king put a death warrant on him." But if we put ourselves in David's sandals for a moment, it becomes downright horrific. For me, it's like the president of the United States telling the CIA, the FBI, and the entire military, "Go get me that crazy Christian guy, Craig Groeschel. I want his sorry carcass, dead or alive." (Now you understand why I still check behind shower curtains!) Wherever you live, imagine that the most powerful leader in your nation issued that command *about you*. Imagine that every force in the country is out scouring the countryside for you, interrogating your friends and your family, hot on your trail. You can't go to any public places. You're always looking over your shoulder.

This nightmare was the reality of David's life. No matter where he went, he couldn't escape his knowledge that the most powerful man in Israel wanted him dead. In Psalm 56:1 – 4, we get a glimpse not only into his ordeal but into how he faced it: "My enemies are in hot pursuit ... My adversaries pursue me all day long; in their pride many are attacking me. *When I am afraid, I put my trust in you.* In God, whose word I praise — in God I trust and am not afraid. What can mere mortals do to me?" (emphasis mine).

David clearly was overwhelmed and perhaps even terrified. But he just called it like it was, being honest with God. He was God's anointed, God's chosen, the future king, but that certainly didn't have any bearing on his circumstances. You can do the same thing David did. It's okay to admit that you're afraid. Name your fears. Just say, "Here's what's happening, God. Here's what I'm afraid of":

"I'm afraid my spouse might be having an affair."
"I'm afraid one of my kids might get a terminal disease."
"I'm afraid my best friend might betray me."
"I'm afraid my business might go under next year."

Then follow that with what David did. "But even though I'm afraid, God, I'm choosing to trust in you." Take it just as far as David did. Say it aloud. Write it down. Rehearse it. Refer to it to remind yourself. Say it over and over: "I believe your Word, God. I'm choosing to trust in you, God. Because of you, I'm choosing not to be afraid."

Examining this passage further, notice the last thing David says here: "What can mere mortals do to me?" Well, let's answer that question. Honestly, what could mortal men have done to him? Well, for starters, they could have killed him! Perhaps even worse, mortal men could have captured him, tortured him, imprisoned him, and made the rest of his life miserable. These all sound pretty horrible.

So if all that's true, then how was David able to overcome his fears? By refocusing his view of the problem, shifting his fear-fueled thoughts from the temporary, earthly point of view to an eternal perspective. By stepping back and viewing his fear from a more comprehensive perspective, David could say, "You know what? Even if my worst what-ifs come to pass, if I still choose to trust God, no one can do anything that hurts me eternally. Nothing." Suddenly his worst what-if paled in comparison with the goodness and faithfulness of God.

What about you? What's your greatest fear? Can you choose to trust God with it? Be as honest with yourself as you can. This is really important. In my experience, the farther away I get from God, the more the what-ifs of this world begin to pile on, trying to suffocate me with fear. But the closer I am to God, the more I'm able to trust him, and the less hold the things of this world have on me. Choose. Tell God what it is you're afraid of. Then trust him no matter what.

Fearless Pursuit

The second tactic for overcoming your fears is directly related to the first. Simply put, you must seek God. That's it. Start seeking God, and don't stop. When you diligently, consistently, tirelessly seek him, your fears will evaporate. Jeremiah 29:12 – 13 says, "You will call on me and come and pray to me, and I will listen to you. You will seek me and find me when you seek me with all your heart."

You might be thinking, "But where can I find him?" Start in his Word. Call out to him in prayer. Seek him with your friends who also follow Christ. Ask them to pray for you. Ask them to pray that God will reveal himself to you, and that he'll show you the path to overcoming your fears. Don't stop. Day and night. Every time you think of it. If you wake up in the night, pray. Get a Bible app for your mobile phone, and anytime you find yourself waiting for an appointment or standing in line, take it out and read. Don't stop. Seek God.

You can find tremendous, life-changing power in David's words in Psalm 34:4: "I sought the LORD, and he answered me; he delivered me from all my fears." Think about those words. Take them to heart. I looked for God — and he delivered me. He delivered me from every fear I had. They're gone. I'm released from all the things that were holding me hostage. He delivered me from them. They're gone, and I'm free.

When you sense fearful emotions are trying to overtake you, try doing just what he did. Who made all of this? Who's in control? Whose promise is it that he will work in "all things" for the good of those who love him (Rom. 8:28)? In those very first moments when you start to feel fear creeping in, close your eyes and picture God on his throne, seated directly between you and your fear. Your fears try to get between you and God. Force them back where they belong. See God between you and them.

When I look at my schedule and I see what's looming in the months ahead, I can feel those old familiar fears about the future starting to slip back in, like shadows trying to eclipse the light. So I close my eyes and start talking to God: "Father, you're enough for today. You've given me everything I need to do everything you want me to do today." Acknowledging that God is in control and seeing him as my protector and my provider has helped me to decisively overcome my fear of the future. He wants to do the same thing for you.

God has not given you a spirit of fear. If you're feeling afraid, that's not from him. Don't accept it. Don't give in to it. What God has given you is a spirit of power, of love, and a sound mind. Seek him. Fear not, for the Lord is with you.

Part 3

TOXIC INFLUENCES

9

Mood Poisoning

Purging the False Promises
of Materialism

That feeling of freedom, open highways of possibilities,
has ... been lost to materialism and marketing.
—Sheryl Crow

A good friend and I were having lunch right after Christmas, and he had just gotten his credit card bill that morning. Talk about a holiday hangover — Visa was *not* everywhere he wanted to be. My buddy complained, "I used to save money throughout the year for Christmas, sort of like what I saw my parents do, and then I didn't have this huge debt come January. While I still try to save, now I'm always playing catch up. It seems like every month has a holiday, special occasion, or gift-giving obligation attached to it." My buddy described month by month in detail where his money went.

Starting with January, he had to pay the bills from the wonderful Christmas his family had just celebrated. In February, there was the piece of jewelry his wife has come to expect for Valentine's Day, as well as gifts for his teenage daughters and twelve-year-old son. March and April bring spring break — they always fly to Florida for some quality beach time — as well as the big family gathering at Easter, which includes a huge meal and Easter baskets for kids and grown-ups alike.

Summer used to provide a financial break, but now his kids' summer camps, his family's week at the lake house for Fourth of July, and their cruise vacation to the Caribbean in August took every penny he had. Come September, it's back to school time, and we all know what that means: new clothes for the kids, new backpacks, and fees for soccer, football, and cheerleading — not to mention new equipment and uniforms. After Halloween (candy, parties, decorations, costumes), it's a downhill slide to Thanksgiving, Black Friday shopping for Christmas presents, and everything leading up to the big day itself. Throw in a handful of birthdays and his wedding anniversary, and my friend had enough expenditures ahead of him to dig quite a hole.

Knowing that I'm rather frugal and adamantly opposed to debt, my buddy wasn't surprised to hear me say, "You know, you don't have to live that way." He looked at me funny for a couple of seconds and said, "But, Craig, *every*body lives that way." I laughed out loud, and fortunately, he did, too. "No," I said. "Not everyone lives that way — it's a choice."

The Price of Admission

I wasn't judging my friend or the millions of people like him who are caught up in the dizzying cycle of work, spend, charge, work harder, spend more, charge more. It's a pervasive, insidious disease, especially in our Western culture and particularly in the US. And it starts at a young age. Kids used to beg for the latest Barbie, G.I. Joe, catcher's mitt, or ten-speed bike. Now they expect iPods, cell phones, and designer clothes, like the mini-adults retailers want them to be.

I know firsthand that the peer pressure to keep up with the latest trends, 2.0 versions, and status symbols starts at an early age. As a product of the Polo and Izod generation, I knew that the cool kids wore shirts with little green alligators on them, unless they were wearing ones with tiny guys swinging a polo mallet on horseback. At my middle school, if you didn't wear the right label, you couldn't hang with the right crowd, which meant you couldn't sit at the right table at lunch, and couldn't go with the right girl to the Valentine's dance. Any shot I had at being junior-high cool hinged on the label inside and the emblem on the front of my shirt.

Though my parents supported my dreams to be cool, they refused to cough up $50 for a shirt that I would outgrow in six months. Rather than simply surrender to a lower-tier, label-less life, I decided to fake it. My mom colluded with me in my clothing masquerade by performing surgery on a pair of Izod socks she picked up at a garage sale. With careful precision, she transplanted the prized reptile onto a plain shirt that cost ten bucks. Our plan almost worked until someone noticed that my alligator was crooked. While I never sat at the cool lunch table again, somehow I survived.

Our culture oozes with toxic materialism. A lying spirit tells the masses that more money and better things are the two tickets we need for admission to the life we desire. If we have the right labels, the new gadgets, the best techno-toys, the latest luxury cars, the nicest custom-built houses, and the fattest 401k's, then we'll be happy, secure, and significant.

Like a smoker enjoying his cigarette, knowing that each puff damages his lungs, many people willingly inhale the toxic lies of materialism at the expense of their souls' health and their effectiveness for Christ in the world. Instead of living with substance and strength, they ingest the lies of materialism and suffer from mood poisoning. When our moods and emotional needs depend on acquiring more possessions, more money, more toys, then we're in for a toxic shock when we find our hands full and our hearts empty. Jesus asked, "What good will it be for someone to gain the whole world, yet forfeit their soul?" (Matt. 16:26).

The Honeymoon's Over

Solomon distilled the essence of the problem in Proverbs 13:7 when he explained that some people like to "pretend to be rich," but in reality, they have nothing. They might own an iPhone, iPad, iPod, but they can't afford to feed their iBody dinner at a restaurant without going into debt. They've believed the lie that more things equal more meaning in life. And our consumer-based, retail-driven economy is more than happy to provide more things to enrich your life every single day of the year. We dive into the pool of poison with a "play now, pay later" mindset.

This is especially true for the younger generation, who've learned bad habits from their parents. According to a recent article, 60 percent of workers under the age of thirty have already cashed in their retirement. A whopping 70 percent of them have no money whatsoever in cash reserves. Nevertheless, they keep spending and charging. Although the generation of twenty- and thirty-somethings has many positive traits, one of the negatives is their spirit of entitlement. I deserve it. Life is short. And I want it now. It's not uncommon for a young couple in their twenties to believe they deserve the same lifestyle as their parents, who worked for thirty years to achieve it.

As a pastor who specialized in ministering to single adults for many years, I helped many couples get married. In our premarital training, we always did some work on finances. Without exception, I always queried about their honeymoon plans. When I'd ask where they were going, almost without fail they'd tell me Hawaii, Cancun, Jamaica, the Bahamas, the Fiji Islands, or some other exotic, tropical, and very expensive island. When I asked them how they'd pay for their dream trip, they'd generally shuffle from side to side, avoiding eye contact. Then one would explain sheepishly that they would charge it on their credit cards and pay it off later.

This always struck me as a sad, and unnecessarily harsh, way to begin a marriage. "Hey, honey, let's go into massive debt that will take years to pay off so we can have this one week of tropical bliss!" You might think I'm trying to kill romance, but it's quite the contrary. I'm convinced that when you're in love, you can enjoy your new spouse anywhere. It's not the destination that makes the trip, but the person you're with. Deep in the heart, genuine, life-changing love makes an ordinary place extraordinary.

To me, it's much more romantic to take a trip you can afford then come home and start your debt-free life together. When Amy and I were married, we had $1,100 saved between the two of us. We knew that we couldn't afford to fly anywhere — not if we wanted to eat when we got there. So we chose to drive my old Honda Accord seven hours to San Antonio, Texas. We stayed in a nice hotel on the River Walk for one night and then at a less expensive hotel a few miles away the rest of the week. We purchased a coupon book that got us meals for half-off. We walked by the river, talked until late at night, and even played card games — not to mention getting to know each other in the biblical sense! We had the time of our lives on a very low-budget, low-frills kind of vacation.

When we ran out of money before our full week was up, we started the seven-hour drive home. Half-way home Amy got the idea to stop and stay at her granddad's vacant trailer home by a pond. So we spent two days enjoying each other in the trailer by the pond, eating peanut butter and jelly sandwiches, and enjoying the time away. And we started our marriage debt free.

Bling Fever

Without even realizing it, so many people today are making a horrible trade. "They exchanged the truth about God for a lie, and worshiped and served created things rather than the Creator — who is forever praised" (Rom. 1:25). This verse captures one of the most toxic exchanges in history. People reject God's truth with its power to liberate and satisfy our souls and instead embrace the pursuit of material items.

Why would Christians (and non-Christians) make such a bad trade? Giving up eternal blessings for temporary and passing ones? Making short-term decisions with long-term consequences? Living for the moment and forgetting about the future? The reason is the false promises — the luxurious lies — of money, materialism, and marketing. Think about it. Money and things make three major promises that they cannot keep: the promises of happiness, significance, and security.

Let's talk about the false promise of happiness. This lie is a strange one, but people believe it by the millions. What's funny about this lie is that you can ask someone, "Does money buy happiness?" Most people I know would say without hesitation, "No, money doesn't buy happiness." But if I then asked them, "Do you think a little more money would make your life better?" they would instinctively respond, "Yes, of course."

Can you see the hypocrisy?

If you look at the way people behave more than at what they say they believe, their actions indicate they believe money and things will make them happy. Husbands break their backs to make more money or acquire more things. Wives go into debt believing the perfect purse, hair color, or bracelet will make their lives better. The just-out-of-college male goes into huge debt buying the new car, convinced it might attract the new wife. It might be the six-figure salary, the kitchen with granite countertops, the walk-in closet, the third-car garage to protect the boat, the newest piece of technology, or the perfect pair of boots that will go with the new jeans you need to get to match the scarf that you didn't purchase but will now that you have the boots. Money and things lie to us. If you have enough, you'll be happy.

Money and things continue to deceive us, promising that if we have enough, we'll be significant. You may not agree at first, but when you think about it, you'll hear echoes of its lying voice. If you have money and nice things, that makes you important. If you don't, you are less than those who do.

Don't believe me? Imagine driving up to see your friends in a twelve-year-old piece-of-junk, ratted-out clunker of a vehicle. Can you feel your embarrassment when the jalopy backfires, then dies, as you open the dented and rusted driver's side door? Contrast that with the feeling you'd have driving a brand new convertible sports car with the top down and music blaring out of the state-of-the-art stereo. Heads turn when you drive in, not because the car almost exploded but because you look hot. Unquestionably, in either car, you are the same person. But the way you feel about yourself likely would be worse in the clunker and better in the shiny sports car. Why? Because you've smoked the culture's cigarette and inhaled the lie.

You might feel better wearing the right pair of jeans, or telling another mom that your kids are in the exclusive private school, or explaining that you live in the neighborhood with the gated entrance. And if you're wearing your no-name jeans, or making excuses why your kids don't go to the exclusive school, or avoiding the name of your gateless neighborhood, could it be that you've believed the lie? Your things and your money don't make you significant, but you believe they do.

Money and things pull another one over on you. These things wrongly promise security. If you are like most people, you tend to think, "If I just had enough money, then I'd feel secure." The problem is that statement is never true. When you get a little more, you feel like you need more. If you ask someone, "How much do you need to feel safe and secure?" the most common response never changes. "I need just a little bit more."

This has been a problem for me my entire life. I've always feared that we wouldn't have enough. Rather than wanting newer and nicer, I've simply wanted more financial padding. You might need some for a rainy day. After getting counseling for my irrational financial fears, I finally admitted the truth. I trusted money to provide more than I trusted God.

Truth-for-One Sale

While a lot of people buy the toxic financial lie and outwardly look like they are happy, significant, and secure, there is another side to the lie — the truth. "And then you will know the truth," Jesus said, "and the truth will set you free" (see John 8:32).

Why do you think our spiritual enemy uses money to deceive? Satan tries to use money as a substitute for God. Remember Jesus said, "No one can serve two masters. Either you will hate the one and love the other, or you will be devoted to the one and despise the other. You cannot serve both God and money" (Matt. 6:24). Notice Jesus didn't say you cannot serve both God and power. Or both God and sex. Or both God and yourself. Jesus specifically highlighted money. You cannot serve both God and money.

Why do you think Jesus focused on dollars? Because money is an appealing, amazingly powerful false god. Our spiritual enemy will use anything to draw our worship away from God. Satan loves when you love and worship money. The toxic trap lures us to worship and serve created things (that which money buys) rather than the Creator who should be forever praised. When you get to its root, what does money do? It promises what only God can provide.

While money promises happiness, true happiness, peace, and joy can be found only in God through Christ. The same is true with significance. Money promises significance, but it doesn't deliver. Only God does. Again, money says if you have enough you'll be secure. But you just need someone you love to get in an accident or have a life-threatening disease to realize all the money in the world can't buy away those troubles. Only God can make you truly secure. We're wrestling with a spiritual problem, not a financial one.

Let's wade through the toxic trash and unearth the truth. Why do you think we trust in money to buy happiness? The reason is simple: because we don't know what we have in Christ. We trust money to make us significant because we don't know who we are in Christ. And we believe money will make us secure because we trust money more than we trust Christ.

Feel the pain of the toxic trap of materialism. In essence, by the way we live, we're saying that what the world offers is better than what Christ offers. Our financial debt is evidence of our distorted beliefs. If you are a Christian, you might put up your defenses. "That's not true!" And out roll the excuses. "My parents didn't teach me about money. My job doesn't pay enough. The economy is bad. My spouse spends too much. I can't help it that my kids need braces. Or that our car broke down. Besides, I'm not as bad as most people. I can't help it if I like nice things."

With few exceptions, if you're in debt, chances are you've swallowed the poisonous pill, believing more would make you happy, significant, or secure. Own it. Don't excuse it. If you didn't believe those lies, why would you have purchased things that you didn't need with money that you didn't have? Our actions reveal what we truly believe: we love, worship, and serve things more than we love, worship, and serve God.

House Rules

So what do we do when we recognize that we've been duped? How do we recover from years of living by a lie? The simple answer is that we need to start living within our means. We need to pay off debt and live as good stewards. But you already knew that, didn't you?

Instead of trying to convince you of the importance of budgeting, saving, and planning (all of which are important and necessary), I'm going to offer something often overlooked that should come before we try to change our behavior. Remember our first problem is a belief problem. Belief overflows to behavior. First we need to change what we believe. When we truly change what we believe, we'll gladly change how we behave.

I'll give you an example. Amy and I have always enjoyed keeping our house nice, especially for company. Years ago, if you called and told me you were coming to visit in an hour, our routine would have looked something like this: I'd run to tell Amy that you were coming. She'd ask when. I'd tell her in an hour. She'd panic. For the next 59.5 minutes we'd run around throwing stuff into a closet and explaining to the kids that "under no circumstances do you open *that* closet!" Then we'd light some candles to give our home that welcoming scent. My job included putting on a worship tape to set the spiritual mood. (If you don't know what a tape is, ask someone over forty.) After freshening up we'd wait for you for the final .5 minutes to put on the our-home-and-family-are-perfect show.

Why do you think we did this? Because our identity was wrapped up in something besides Christ. You could say that we worshiped our image or your opinion of our image. Our actions revealed what we believed. We didn't know who we were or what we had. We believed a toxic lie. Now, there is nothing wrong with keeping your house nice, but when we changed our beliefs, we found a better way to behave.

As Amy matured in Christ, her priorities started to visibly change. I still remember the day Amy approached me with her new idea. "Instead of putting so much emphasis on our home, what if we chose to value relationships over our image?" she asked, revealing her well-thought-out passion. "I'd like for our place to be *the* house!" Amy said, with a spiritual strength that rivaled a Billy Graham sermon. I immediately knew what she was talking about.

She didn't want the house that everyone wanted or the house that won the yard of the month award. Amy wanted something else that I'd never experienced firsthand. Every neighborhood has *the* one house that every kid wants to come to for fun. It's *the* house where everyone spends the most time, creates the most memories, and can't wait to come back to visit. It's *the* house that's never perfect but always full — of food, of love, of people.

Amy carefully explained to me that we could continue to work hard to have the "perfect" house (something that is unattainable anyway), or we could relax our standards and invest more energy in the people we love. So we decided we'd no longer kill ourselves to impress you with our image but instead serve you with our love. We'd have the house that felt like a home.

Now if you come over, chances are pretty good you'll have to walk by a bicycle or two, a rip stick, some faded sidewalk chalk, and a Frisbee in the driveway. You'll step over several toys in the entry way, and the cushions probably won't be straight on our sofa. You might see a half-finished board game sitting out on the dining room table and four stuffed animals sitting in chairs like they're having a tea party. But I promise that although the house may not be perfect, you'll feel welcomed and loved.

When we became more secure with who we were in Christ, we didn't need to impress others with our image but could serve them with our love. When we changed what we believed (valuing people over things), our new beliefs changed how we behaved. And with our new beliefs we found a better way to live. We don't have to live with the constant nausea of materialism; we can be settled and truly full with Living Water and the Bread of Life.

Profit Margin

When you overcome toxic materialistic lies, you discover a better way to live. The truth is that happiness, significance, and security are found in Christ alone. Paul revealed this powerfully from a house prison toward the end of his life. "But whatever were gains to me I now consider loss for the sake of Christ. What is more, I consider everything a loss because of the surpassing worth of knowing Christ Jesus my Lord, for whose sake I have lost all things. I consider them garbage, that I may gain Christ" (Phil. 3:7 – 8).

The word in the original language translated as "garbage" is a strong word. It can be translated as "waste" or "dung," or even a stronger word that you might not expect to find in Scripture. In other words, Paul said all the things that I thought were important are actually good-for-nothing, useless, stinking dog poop (my kids' translation). He knew that money and things would never fulfill him. They were nothing compared with the joy of knowing Christ.

When you grow closer to Christ, the toxic temptations of worldly possessions loosen their grip on you. Instead you care less about this world and more about the one to come. The deceiving culture tells you that if you have more, you'll be satisfied. Charles Spurgeon said it well. "You say, 'If I had a little more I should be very satisfied.' You make a mistake. If you are not content with what you have, you would not be satisfied if it were doubled." Having more of this world never fulfills. Only more of Christ does.

To really heal from the materialistic toxins, I encourage you to say the truth to yourself over and over again.

Money and things will never fulfill me.

Money and things will *never* fulfill me.

Money and things will NEVER fulfill me.

Say it over and over and over and over again, until you believe it. And when you do believe it, you'll begin putting it into practice. Your behavior will change.

Jesus said, "Life does not consist in an abundance of possessions" (Luke 12:15). You are not what you have. You are not where you live. You are not what you wear. You are not what you drive.

If you are not all those things, then who are you?

You are who God says you are. You are his child. You are a joint heir with Christ.

And because you belong to God, "his divine power has given us everything we need for a godly life" (2 Peter 1:3). You have everything you need to do everything God wants you to do. You are complete in him.

When you truly believe that, you start to live the better life. Proverbs 15:16 says, "Better a little with the fear of the Lord than great wealth with turmoil." It is better to have some with God than have a lot with tension, fighting, and fear. A little with God is better.

Proverbs 15:17 says, "Better a small serving of vegetables with love than a fattened calf with hatred." It's better to eat a salad with those you love than have a steak after you divorce. Again, with God, life is better.

Solomon said it is "better to be a nobody and yet have a servant than pretend to be somebody and have no food" (Prov. 12:9). It is better to not fake it but live within your means and not worry about money and things. There is a better way to live.

We will never discover lasting happiness, significance, and security in the temporary things of this world because we weren't made to live a temporary life. That's why we should lower our expectations of earth. Earth is not heaven. It was never meant to be. No new car, new house, new living room furniture, new kitchen appliances, new clothes, new hair, new baby, new vacation, new job, new income, new husband, or new anything will ever satisfy us, because we were not made for the things of this world.

Someone said it's not wrong to have things. It's wrong when your things have you. If you fight hard against the current of commercialism, you can swim to better waters. Stop believing the lie. More money and things will not make your life any more meaningful. But the Son of God, the risen Christ, will.

10

Germ Warfare

Cleansing Our Lives
of Cultural Toxins

*For the first time, the weird and the stupid and
the coarse are becoming our cultural norm,
even our cultural ideal.*
—Carl Bernstein

I've already shared how going to the movies can be a spiritual exercise in self-control and forgiveness as I encounter the many people there intent on crowding, talking, and spoiling my entertainment. You'll also recall how I learned the hard way a few years ago to be more discerning about the films I choose to see. So now that I'm more discerning about what I see, I tend to rely on the recommendations of friends, other church staff members, as well as internet sources and apps that assess movies and their content.

Recently, when I asked a friend for recommendations of a good movie to rent, he responded enthusiastically, "Have you seen *The Hangover*? It may be the funniest movie I've ever seen!" Excited about a potentially great comedy, I asked a couple of my staff members about the movie. They too had seen it and said it was a riot and a must-see.

Since I wasn't sure what *The Hangover* was rated, my last checkpoint was a little research to see if this was a movie for the whole family or one for just me and Amy to watch together. What I discovered floored me. According to *www.screenit.com*, this comedy has more than its fair share of non-family-friendly scenes, intense language, and sexual situations. The rough spots include ninety-one variations of the F-bomb (apparently it can function as noun, verb, adjective — maybe even a conjunction for all I know), forty-one excretory words, fourteen references to a person's behind, thirteen "hells," and nine slang terms for male anatomy. To top it all off, this hilarious movie has thirty-one versions of taking God's name in vain. Not exactly the Baskin-Robbins "thirty-onederful" flavors I was looking for.

Bombs Away

When I told my friends and staff members that the movie had ninety-one F-bombs, which averages out to approximately one version of the F-word per minute, they were all shocked. "Really? I didn't even notice" was the most common response.

Really, you didn't notice one F-word each minute?

Maybe you've seen the movie and don't think the language or sex scenes are a big deal. Maybe you're rolling your eyes (well, meta-phorically) and thinking, "Aren't you going a little overboard? Who sits through a movie and counts the cuss words? Come on, Craig— lighten up! Nobody takes a comedy seriously."

Please understand that I've seen my share of *The Hangover*-ish movies. As a child of the '80s, I grew up on a diet of movies like *Fast Times at Ridgemont High, Risky Business,* and *Porky's.* It's not that I'm particularly proud of this cultural education (I'd probably leave this list off my resume if ever applying for a job as a pastor), but I'm no teetotaling separatist who watches only *Veggie Tales.*

You might be like a lot of people who say, "Profanity, violence, and sex in the movies don't really bother me. If it doesn't bother me, it must not be that big of a deal." Remember, I used to think this way too. If you're a Christian, though, wouldn't you agree that there has to be a boundary somewhere? A way to discern what pleases God and moves us closer to him instead of farther away? And can we trust our own sensibilities to know what's truly best for us? Can you really endure an onslaught of F-bombs in a movie and not get wounded?

Consider, for example, if I dropped ninety-one F-bombs in my sermon this Sunday; do you think that no one in my church would care? Chances are good that I'd stir up a bit of controversy to say the least. So if you agree that ninety-one is too many F-words for a Sun-day sermon, then how about fifty? Or twenty-three?

What's the magic number? Most people in my church would say

that even one F-bomb would be too many, much less taking God's name in vain. Yet the majority of them paid good money to be entertained by some form of media containing the same language or much worse within the past thirty days.

So let's wrestle with this subject. If it's not okay for me or you to say certain words or make particular jokes or references in church, then why would it be right for Christians to pay their hard-earned money to be entertained by something similar?

I agree that context makes a difference. You attend church (I hope) to worship God, hear his Word preached, and fellowship with others, not to be entertained. Conversely, you go to the movies or download Netflix to escape and enjoy yourself, not to meet God and get spiritually nourished.

There's only one problem with this line of reasoning. Our lives are not so neatly compartmentalized just because we're in a different setting for a different purpose. We aren't machines with software programs that can sort and file things away, separate from all the other parts of the system. It's tempting to think that what we watch on TV, see at the movies, listen to on our iPods, play on our gaming systems, and read before bedtime doesn't affect us.

But it does. Each image and message we ingest may be a germ that will make us gravely ill, especially when combined with the many other sensory germs we're taking in. If we're serious about our spiritual house cleaning, then there must be no exceptions. We must take the images, language, and stories we allow into our minds and hearts very seriously. We must disinfect our hearts with the germ-killing power of the truth.

Pain Threshold

Movies, media, and culture are not bad in themselves. But consuming spiritually toxic material from our culture without discernment can kill you. People in our culture don't have the same standards, priorities, or responsibilities that we as Christians have. If pleasing God is not their focus, why should they care what they put in a movie, song, TV show, magazine article, or book?

I'm not saying that God's truth is found only in what self-proclaimed Christians produce in our culture. He uses everything and anything he wants to draw people into relationship with him. But generally speaking, most cultural elements can be placed on a continuum.

A few might be helpful to you spiritually, building your faith and drawing you closer to God and his mission for you on earth. Some may be neutral and range from slightly entertaining to an utter waste of time, while others slowly seep poison into your soul. It could be the music you enjoy on your iPod or the sites you visit on the internet. Some are harmless. Others deadly.

However, we rarely recognize the negative impact of the cultural diet we consume daily. Like a dieter with a new bag of potato chips, we start with one or two and suddenly find ourselves thirsty with an empty bag in our hands. No one wakes up in the morning and says, "I think I'll waste the entire day playing graphically violent video games, watching pornographic movies, and listening to profanity-laced music." The subtlety of our media-saturated society is its pervasive influence. We take it in all the time, and little by little we become desensitized to harmful, ungodly material one pixel at a time.

For example, the first time I watched Ultimate Fighting, I honestly turned my head several times. Two guys kicked, punched, and wrestled each other in a locked cage until one was clearly nearer to death than the other. Blood poured from one guy's eye as he was pinned on the ground. His attacker sensed an opportunity and sent elbow after elbow into his face, bouncing the poor guy's head off the floor like a basketball player dribbling a ball down the court.

Suddenly, the guy on the bottom miraculously rolled his hips and wrapped a leg around his attacker's arm, pinning him in a human vise. Then I couldn't believe my eyes and ears as I watched the one guy brutally snap his opponent's arm into two pieces. Not only could you hear the *pop!* but the victim's broken bone virtually burst out of his skin. "Uhhgghh!" I shouted and turned away, feeling like I might gag on the bile rising in my throat.

Yet as gross and as wrong as that seemed to me, I was strangely drawn to it. The next time I watched a similar fight, I still winced at the violent blows, but somehow it didn't seem quite as bad. Sure, the fight was brutal and there was still a lot of blood. But my perspective changed. "This is not that bad." Each time I watched it, the brutality didn't seem quite as bad.

Now, years and dozens of fights later, I'm the first to shout, "Snap his arm!" as I watch the fights with my two sons. (Yes, Amy and I have had many discussions about why I allow them to watch this and she doesn't.) What's happened? The fighting hasn't changed. It's my standards that have changed. What used to bother me, disturb me, and upset me has now become entertainment to me.

Pooped Out

If we want to purify our hearts and lives, then we must begin by recognizing the various toxins and their point of entry into our lives. When it comes to anything we consume, a little bit of poison goes a long way. The apostle Paul explained this truth in a letter to his friends in Corinth. The Corinthian church was filled with well-intentioned Christians who'd fallen victim to countless cultural temptations. Paul asked them bluntly, "Don't you know that a little yeast leavens the whole batch of dough? Get rid of the old yeast, so that you may be a new unleavened batch — as you really are" (1 Cor. 5:6 – 7).

Yeast in the Bible often represents sin, so Paul clearly isn't pulling any punches. (I wonder if he'd be a fan of Ultimate Fighting? Okay, maybe not.) Essentially he's asking, "Can't you see that your sinfulness is taking over? A little bit of sin — or poison — goes a long way to destroy a life. Get rid of the sin so you can live without it as God intends."

Here's the best illustration that I know of this timeless truth. A loving mother demonstrated this principle to her son, Cade. When his friends invited him over to watch a movie, one just released on DVD and rated PG-13, Cade begged his mom to let him see it. His mom asked him her usual questions, "Buddy, is it a good movie? One that won't hurt your Christian walk?"

Knowing it had some less than appropriate scenes, Cade shuffled from one foot to the other and searched for the right words. Not wanting to lie to his mom, he tried to walk on the edge of the truth. "Well, it's not as bad as a lot of movies," he said enthusiastically. "And all my friends have seen it. There's only a little bit of bad stuff in it." He held his breath, awaiting his mom's final verdict on his movie-going fate.

His mom smiled and said, "Well, of course, honey. As long as there's only 'a little bit of bad stuff in it.'" Cade was stunned! Before she changed her mind, the grateful teen bolted for his room, texted his friends the good news, then lost himself in his favorite iPad game.

Now if you're a parent, you probably already know that Cade's mom had something up her sleeve. She headed to the kitchen and started implementing her plan. Selecting her son's favorite brownie mix from the pantry, she added the requisite water, eggs, and oil, stirring the mixture together in a big white bowl. While the oven preheated, Cade's crafty mom strolled into the back yard for her secret ingredient. Searching carefully in the grass, she scooped up something that their dog Ginger had recently left behind.

She returned to the kitchen, stirred in a teaspoon of Ginger's secret ingredient, poured the thick, chocolate batter into a nonstick pan, and set the oven timer for twenty minutes. Just as she pulled the brownies from the oven, Cade bounced down the stairs right on cue.

"Do I smell my favorite brownies?" he asked with excitement.

"You bet!" his mom said, smiling. After letting them cool for a few moments, Cade's mom cut into the warm brownies and plopped a large one on his plate. Just as his fork hit the plate, she stopped him, and mentioned casually, "Just so you know, I added a special ingredient this time." She paused without cracking a smile. "I put a teaspoon of Ginger's poop in your brownies."

"What?!" Cade shouted, immediately disgusted. "Mom, are you crazy? Why'd you do that?" he choked while pushing his plate away.

Cade's mom went to the fridge and poured her son his usual glass of milk. "Don't worry, buddy. I didn't put a lot of poop in the brownies. There's just a little bit of bad stuff."

He rolled his eyes, but she'd made her point and served it up home-style. Cade realized he wouldn't be seeing the movie.

The moral of this story? A little bit of poop goes a long way.

Ask yourself, is there a little bit of poop in the media you normally enjoy? Do your friends lead you into places or situations that stink? How about the television shows you watch regularly? Think back over what you've watched this past week. Pick a show, any show. How about *The Bachelor*? Besides all the skin and overnight sex partners, what subtle (or not so subtle) messages does this show send? The answers: (1) everyone is hot, (2) love is best found on helicopters flying over waterfalls, and (3) if you can't decide who to marry, spend the night having sex with all three before deciding not to marry any of them. Okay, sorry — I admit I'm not a fan of the show, though you have to give me points for having sat through an episode.

How about the romance novels on the bestseller lists? What's their message? The shirtless ripped guy who cleans your pool will sweep you off your feet and you'll have sex by the pool for the rest of your life. Don't read romance novels? How about *Maxim*? What's the message? You should have six-pack abs so you can enjoy sex with at least three girls a week. What you consume may have just a little poison. But as you know, a little poison goes a long way.

Mom Was Right

You have to admit, our parents must've been on the debate team at some point. Where else would they learn the classic line, "If everyone else jumped off a cliff, would you? Just because everyone else is doing it doesn't make it right." Now I get goose bumps when I hear myself say that exact same thing to one of our kids. I have to admit, Mom was right.

I like the way Eugene Peterson renders Romans 12:2 in *The Message*: "Don't become so well-adjusted to your culture that you fit into it without even thinking. Instead, fix your attention on God. You'll be changed from the inside out. Readily recognize what he wants from you, and quickly respond to it. Unlike the culture around you, always dragging you down to its level of immaturity, God brings the best out of you, develops well-formed maturity in you."

It's so easy to become a cultural chameleon and blend in, conform, and become like the culture around you. And as your discernment becomes camouflaged by cultural standards, your spiritual priorities will disappear. If you don't want to disappear into the worldly culture, then you must be willing to stand out.

You can let culture drag you down, or you can ask God to pull you up. Don't be fooled by what's popular and considered acceptable by most. Remember what Jesus said in Matthew 7:13 – 14: "For wide is the gate and broad is the road that leads to destruction, and many enter through it. But small is the gate and narrow the road that leads to life, and only a few find it." The crowd follows the wide-open road. Only a few are on the right path. Which one are you traveling?

We have to acknowledge that the majority isn't always right. Just because everyone else does something doesn't make it right. Even if everyone else believes watching, reading, surfing, or listening to something is acceptable, you'll be wise to stop and ask God if this is his best for you.

As believers in Christ, we are called to live a holy life. We're instructed to "be holy" because God is holy (1 Peter 1:16). The Greek word translated as "holy" is *hagios*, which means "to be set apart" or "to be different." It carries an inherent contrast and can be translated "to be like the Lord and different from the world." If we're not any different, maybe it's because we don't know Christ or we aren't living out the commitment we made to know him.

Consumer Reports

A wise person told me, "Just because you *could* do something doesn't mean you *should*." And the truth is that we have tremendous freedom in Christ. If we're only trying to "follow the rules" so we can feel good about what great Christians we are, then we're missing the point, not to mention much of the joy in life. We must learn how to discern, balancing the freedom we have in Christ with the clear standards God gives us for being set apart in a sinful world.

For example, could I break the law and drive twenty miles per hour over the speed limit and still go to heaven when I die? Of course I could. Should I? No, but I could. Or could I eat tons of junk food, never exercise, and become lazy, obese, and out of shape and still love Jesus? The answer is yes, I could. Should I? Again, this wouldn't be wise. How about one more? Could I go into massive debt buying tons of things that I can't afford and wade into deep financial waters and still be a follower of Jesus? Obviously, I could. But should I? No. Just because you could doesn't mean you should.

In other words, even if you have the freedom to do something that won't kill you, it doesn't mean that it's wise. Paul, speaking again to the Corinthian believers, said, "'Everything is permissible for me' — but not everything is beneficial. 'Everything is permissible for me' — but I will not be mastered by anything" (1 Cor. 6:12 NIV 1984 ed.).

Let's apply this principle to the media we consume. Could I read an article in *Cosmo* magazine called "Forty-three Ways to Drive Your Lover Wild in Bed"? Yes. Should I? You be the judge. How about skimming through the pages of *GQ*? Should I spend my time obsessing over the latest men's fashions and staring at ads of mostly naked women? Be honest. Is that how God wants you to invest the life he gave you? Can you watch *Desperate Housewives* and be entertained by who's sleeping with whom on Wisteria Lane this week? Sure. Should you?

Some people disagree with me, but I refuse to take a legalistic stance and draw a hard line based on someone else's standards. For example, when it comes to movies, I've heard respected Christian leaders say, "Going to see an R-rated movie is *always* wrong." Or other people say a Christian should never listen to secular music. That's a stupid and legalist line to draw. While I understand their intention, I also believe that a maturing Christian adult should have enough wisdom to decide what movie (or any other cultural influence) is helpful or hurtful.

The fact that we're called to discernment and not indoctrination is crucial to understand. *The Passion of the Christ* earned an R rating for its brutal violence, yet most Christians agree the movie has tremendous spiritual value. But at the same time, there needs to be a line somewhere. As you pray, I believe God will show you where to draw the line.

So you might ask, "How do I know what influences are good and which are bad?" Glad you asked. Sometimes it may be really obvious. If someone invites you to see a movie called *The Virgin Suicides* or *Hell's Revenge*, the title alone should probably serve as fair warning. When your buddy from school invites you to do vodka shots before going to a Lord of Death concert, you'll want to think twice. If your priority is a pure life, then you should skip that party.

But you'll be faced with many situations that are not nearly as obvious. I've heard people say, "Let your conscience be your guide." If you don't feel bad about it, why not enjoy it? This sounds logical and often is — but not always. Here's the problem. The Bible says that your conscience can be seared (see 1 Tim. 4:2). Think about a nice juicy steak being seared on the grill. If you leave that fillet on the grill too long, it's going to be as tough and dry as shoe leather, no matter how tender it was before. After enough wrong behavior or influences, a person's conscience is no longer an accurate guide.

I've heard some people defend what they watch, read, or enjoy by saying, "[Fill in the blank] doesn't bother me." Maybe violence doesn't bother them. Or cussing doesn't bother them. Or racy humor doesn't bother them. Just because something doesn't bother you doesn't mean that it shouldn't.

Others have said, "If something makes you happy, then it must not be that bad." The problem? When happiness becomes our standard for judging truth, things that make us happy give us permission to do some things that otherwise would be considered wrong. For example, when Christian couples marry, they generally vow to God to stay married "for better or for worse." Yet often times when one spouse isn't happy, they justify leaving the marriage to pursue happiness. Why? It could be they've seen it on *Desperate Housewives*, read about it in *Cosmopolitan*, or had three other friends who all did the same thing. Happy doesn't make it right.

If it's not always clear what is good and what isn't, what should we do? I'd suggest you err on the safe side. If I offered you some water from a well and told you there is an 80 percent chance it's not poisonous, you'd probably look for some bottled water instead. Play it safe. It's better to be safe than sorry. (Sorry, I just sounded like your mom again.)

There are two short Bible verses that offer the best guidance. First Thessalonians tells us, "Test everything. Hold on to the good. Avoid every kind of evil" (5:21 – 22 NIV 1984 ed.). Test everything. If you find good, God-honoring content, material, or lyrics, then hold on to it. If it's truly helpful, enjoy it. But if there is even a little bit of poop, something toxic and hurtful to your soul, avoid it. Get away from it. Turn it off. Put it down. Walk away. Leave the building. Change channels. "Run, Forrest, run!" Don't expose yourself to anything that will distract you from God's best.

As you discern, here are three questions to ask yourself:

1. *Am I being entertained by sin?* Is this article, book, show, website, or movie sinful? Just because something is entertaining doesn't mean it's good for you. Just because something is funny doesn't make it right. Just because it helps you relax doesn't mean it is the right way to relax. Imagine if I told you a very funny racist joke. Would my joke be appropriate just because it's funny? Funny doesn't make wrong right.

2. *Is this pleasing to God?* In case you forget who God is, he is the all-knowing, ever-present, all-powerful Creator and Sustainer of the universe. He is so holy he cannot look upon evil (see Hab. 1:13). Our lives should bring glory and honor to God. If it doesn't honor God, don't consume it.

3. *Does this lure me away from Christ?* Is what I'm consuming drawing me closer to Christ or taking me away from him? If the latter, then I don't want to have anything to do with it.

White Balance

If you don't think anything is wrong with all the cultural influences that invade your life daily, chances are that you're interpreting right and wrong through a distorted lens. Our church shoots videos every week to use in different areas of ministry. Every time one of our video team members records me, we hold up a white piece of paper in front of the camera before starting. This shot is called a white balance.

We do this each time because the camera can't interpret colors until it sees true white. Without a white balance, a blue shirt could look grey or a red flag could appear orange. Once the camera sees true white, it knows how to discern all the other colors. Once you see pure white — or truth — you can see clearly that so much of what we take in is hurtful to us and displeasing to God.

This chapter may be hitting you hard about now. If you're taking this message seriously, you might be rethinking some of your daily consumption habits. You might even be thinking, "Oh great! So now I can't watch my favorite show. Or read my favorite book. Or surf my favorite sites. What am I going to do with my time?" I can't be your conscience. But allow me to make a few suggestions on some healthy ways to spend the time that's been devoted to an unhealthy diet. How about spending some time with your kids. Serve in your church. Volunteer in your community. Mentor someone. Visit a hospital or nursing home. Lead a small group. Open up God's Word. Replace those nasty cultural germs with life-giving habits that restore a clean soul.

Think about how different your life will be when you stop consuming things with a little bit of poop. Instead, allow God's Word and the guidance of his Holy Spirit to reset your white balance, to readjust your standard of right and wrong, and to live in a manner that brings glory and honor to God.

11

Radioactive
Relationships

Loving Unhealthy People without Getting Sick

Associate with men of good quality if you esteem your own reputation; for it is better to be alone than in bad company.

—George Washington

Think about your relatives for a moment. Who is the difficult one in your family? Maybe it's your mother-in-law. She seems normal at times but then has these crazy spells that make you want to wear a straightjacket and be placed in a padded cell. She might talk non-stop

195

about all the cute little things your spouse did as a child even when it's clear that your spouse hates to be reminded. Or maybe she ignores one grandchild's birthday and dotes on another one. She might wear loud colors and chew gum and play bingo excessively. Perhaps she steals the salt and pepper shakers every time you go to a restaurant or orders matching outfits from the Home Shopping Network for every member of your family.

Or maybe it's your cousin. You know, the one that's the offspring of the Munsters and the Addams families, a cross between Cousin Eddie and Cousin It. He makes people uncomfortable just by showing up, a creepy grin on his face for no reason, always eager to discuss his favorite cable show (usually something like *Doctor Who* or *Ghost Hunters*). Or maybe it's your nutty aunt who lives in another state and loves cats and crochets baby booties for you (not your children) each Christmas even though you graduated from college years ago.

Yes, every family has one, a psycho, tough-to-deal-with sort of deranged person who makes life challenging for everyone around them. They may be angry or silly, defensive or detached, petty or delusional, shrill or sullen, whiny or saccharine, bitter or baffling, critical or indulgent — or all of the above! They make passive-aggressive look like a new form of martial arts and could use their old mood ring as a traffic light it changes so often.

Every family possesses at least one off-the-charts challenging person. If you're tempted to tell me that yours doesn't, then I hate to be the one to break it to you, but maybe *you* are the one!

Toxic Tag-Alongs

While I'm exaggerating a bit, you have to admit that the people around us can be a great blessing or they can be extremely difficult. Our family, friends, and co-workers can be life-giving, loving, and inspiring, or they can be life-draining, hateful, and depressing. Consider the circle of people in your life. Do you have someone in your life who encourages you, lifts you up, and leads you closer to Christ? If you do, then give thanks and take every opportunity you can to enjoy their company. You'd be wise to spend time with those people who make you better.

On the other hand, you may spend a lot of time around someone who takes you in the opposite direction. Instead of making you feel better, this person always picks you apart, finding fault in most of what you do. Rather than lifting you, they drag you down, making sure you feel bad about yourself and life in general. They are negative, critical, belittling. Perhaps they manipulate your feelings or tempt you with things that hurt your soul. They may enjoy filling your mind with doubts and half-truths about yourself, other people, or even God. Some people are helpful. Others can be the worst toxic influence you face in life.

The people closest to you will hands down be your greatest spiritual asset or your worst spiritual curse. Those you spend the most time with can propel you closer to God, serving him faithfully and pleasing him in all you do. Or toxic tag-alongs (sounds like some kind of spoiled Girl Scout cookie) can corrupt your good intentions and rob you of the blessings God wants to pour out on you. After you've swum in their poisonous presence, they leave you sitting in a puddle of sewage, nursing a corroded soul.

Bad Blood

You might not think it really matters who you spend time with. You are your own person, right? Others don't make you who you are. While it is true that others can't control you, it is also true that others can (and do) influence you. It's tempting to think you can help, or even rescue, those playing in the gutter of their toxic lifestyles. In some cases, you'll be able to assist and encourage these individuals. But if the majority of your close relationships are with people living a life displeasing to God, more often than not, they will bring you down long before you bring them up.

The Bible says clearly and directly, "Do not be misled: 'Bad company corrupts good character'" (1 Cor. 15:33). I'm guessing Paul began with "do not be misled" because when it comes to hanging out with the wrong kind of people, so many of us can become misled, then tolerant, then corrupted by those around us. It sounds like a no-brainer — toxic people will make us sick too — but in the midst of real-life relationships, it can be hard to see. And even when we're aware of a dysfunctional relationship, it can be hard to do something about it.

Just tonight we were riding home from church when my youngest son, Stephen (whom we affectionately call Bookie), called his little sister a "bumbling blockhead." When I asked him where he heard the phrase, he told me that a boy in his church class taught him that name. Then Bookie told me several other names the other boy said that Bookie knew he probably shouldn't ever say. Did my son lift the other boy out of his bad name-calling? Not quite. Instead, Bookie quickly jumped down to his level and joined in the name-calling game. Why? Bad company corrupts good character.

Earlier this year I spent time counseling a couple whose lives had been devastated by an affair. The husband — I'll call him Sean — was known in the community as a strong Christian but had made some tragically sinful mistakes and engaged in a sexual relationship with a younger woman at his office. When I asked him what happened, Sean recounted a long history of how he started going out for drinks after work with his co-workers. At first, he thought he could be a witness to those who didn't know Christ. While they drank beer and wine, he enjoyed a glass of ice water (with a lime just for kicks). They'd tease him about being a "Jesus freak" or a "choir boy" and then criticize the people they knew who claimed to be Christians.

Before long, though, Sean found himself slipping into their behavior rather than pulling them to his. He started laughing at their inappropriate jokes and enjoying their sexual innuendoes. He occasionally would criticize a church in town and other Christians. He wanted to belong and didn't want to be seen as different or weird. What once bothered Sean started to intrigue him.

After constant prodding, he joined his friends in "adult beverages." Instead of water, he drank Coronas (still with a lime — just for kicks). And even though Sean loved his wife, one of the younger women in the group loved to flirt with him, especially when they had

had a few drinks. One thing led to another, and now this man and his broken wife sat before me trying to pick up the jagged shards of a shattered marriage. Bad company corrupts.

Paul, in dealing with toxic people, warned Timothy, his spiritual son in the faith, to "avoid godless chatter, because those who indulge in it will become more and more ungodly. Their teaching will spread like gangrene" (2 Tim. 2:16 – 17). I don't know if you've ever seen gangrene, but it's one nasty disease. The flesh-eating ordeal starts as a small, simple infection. But then blood stops flowing to that infected part, and the body rots. The disease cruelly eats away at the flesh, which decays a little more day by day.

Not a pretty picture, but an accurate one of what our souls will suffer if we aren't careful about our relationships. The Bible tells us to stay far away from discussions that are ungodly, or we too will decay and rot morally, becoming more and more ungodly. Bad company is toxic to your soul. The wrong relationships corrupt, pollute, infect, rot, and destroy good character.

Toxic Trinity

Based on my experiences and observations, I see three common types of toxic people. They can be found in most any family, office, church, or neighborhood. The first are those I call the *chronic critics*. These are the people who can find fault in everything — and I do mean *everything.* It's too hot or too cold, too rainy or too dry; the weather's always bad. The car sounds funny and it's really too old anyway; it needs new tires and the upholstery's splitting.

They pick at you like a scab, and nothing you do is right. That haircut you got looks a little ragged, and you probably paid too much for it too. That church service is too dull. Or maybe it is too "entertaining" and the worship is too "rock 'n' roll." The meal is not what they ordered, plus it's cold anyway. The person you're dating is a loser who's never going to marry you. The movie is boring and stupid with bad acting and a predictable plot. And on and on and on, day after day, year after year.

The chronically negative person wears on you, dragging you down day by negative day. Their criticism is never constructive. Their judgmental spirit clogs your heart. Their gossip infects your opinion of others. Some have the spiritual gift of encouragement; these people have the unholy gift of complaining.

After God delivered the Israelites from slavery, they fell into the chronically negative category. God performed miracle after miracle and blessed them beyond measure, but nothing was good enough for them. At least fourteen times in Exodus and Numbers, the Israelites whine, "I wish we had never left Egypt. I'm sick of this food. We'll never reach the Promised Land. Why are we out here? This is taking forever. It would have been better if we'd just died." Blah, blah, blah, blah. Over time, the chronically negative can pull down even the most positive soul.

The second type of toxic person is the *controller*. Controllers are overbearing, forcing their way and opinions upon you regardless of your will. It might seem small and insignificant at first — going to their favorite restaurant or movie. Before long they are choosing your college, your girlfriend, and your future career. If you're married to a controller, you might feel like you are losing your personal identity. You're barely able to make even the simplest decisions for yourself, always surrendering to avoid a fight. Your spouse knows how to manipulate, wielding fear and guilt as weapons that threaten your soul.

One young lady confessed to me that she loved worshiping God at church but feared her father would find out she was here. Even though she was thirty-two, a wife, and the mother of three kids, her father, who lived in another state, forbade her to go to a church outside of his chosen denomination. For her whole life, the woman's dad fought to control what she did. Controllers may have good intentions, but their darts are poisonous.

Finally, the third type of toxic person is the *tempter*. This type encourages you to do things that you know you shouldn't and may not normally even want to do. It might be your boyfriend who pushes you to do things sexually, although you've made it clear that you'd rather save that for marriage. Or it might be your buddy who smokes two packs a day and lures you back into the old destructive lifestyle you fought so valiantly to leave behind. It could be your rich friend who lives for material things. Though you know there is more to life than possessions, each time you're close to your blingy-friend, you crave what she has. Or maybe it is your old high school buddies you reconnected with on Facebook. They're not horrible people, but they invite you to go partying with them and you know where that one-way street leads.

One of my close friends is a firefighter. This Christian servant loves his wife and strives to honor her with sexual purity in every way. Yet every day he goes to work, he's surrounded by tempters. His station buddies aren't ax murderers or child molesters. They're just everyday guys who like to talk about what everyday guys enjoy — sex. Without Christian principles to slow their sexual appetites, these men surround themselves with porn, porn, and more porn. My friend spends twenty-four hours at a time with toxic tempters testing his tenacity for truth.

Good Fences

If you're becoming aware of a toxic relationship with potential to poison your life, don't panic. The good news is that God's Word is full of life-giving examples and instructions on how to love your friends and family back to health. First, we begin by learning to set healthy boundaries. Just like a rancher surrounds his property and livestock with a fence, we too should put protective measures in place to protect from bad influences. What does a properly placed fence do? It keeps the bad out and the good in. Our boundaries will help us to enjoy the good people without inhaling the bad.

If you think that sounds unnecessary, realize that even Jesus regularly set boundaries. Our Savior loved everyone equally, but he didn't treat everyone equally. There's a big difference. For example, Jesus recruited twelve disciples, not twelve hundred or twelve thousand. Although he loved the whole world with the same godlike unconditional love, he didn't select everyone in the whole world to be in his inner circle.

You may also notice that when Jesus entered a village, crowds gathered hoping for miracles. Jesus often healed a handful of people, but he didn't always heal everyone's needs. With some people, he made his boundaries explicitly clear, especially with the Pharisees. Almost every time you see the hypocritical Pharisees interacting with Jesus, the Son of God takes control and puts the Pharisees in their place — a few times almost brutally. The harder the legalistic zealots shoved their agenda on Jesus, the harder he pushed back with God's truth, and the stronger and bigger he built his boundaries. Jesus fenced some out, placing boundaries for higher purposes.

Even those closest to Jesus hit a wall every now and then. When Jesus' friend and disciple Peter tried to talk Jesus out of giving his life, Jesus turned and said to Peter, "Get behind me, Satan! You are a stumbling block to me; you do not have in mind the concerns of God, but merely human concerns" (Matt. 16:23). No one could distract Jesus from God's agenda, not even his followers.

For the record, I don't recommend that you say to your grandma, "You're gangrene to me. Get behind me, Satan." But what you have to do is be willing to set up boundaries so you can be stronger and better minister to people. Here are two things you can learn to say to help establish healthy boundaries.

First, you can tell people, "I won't let you talk to me or treat me that way." You don't have to run for your life, call people crazy, or hold up a sign that says, "Keep Away!" Instead just talk to people plainly. When someone wants to infect you with destructive gossip, you simply explain, "I'm not participating." (Remember, if someone will gossip to you, they will gossip about you.) Put up a wall. Explain your stance. Hold your ground.

If all your girlfriends constantly trash talk men, tell them, "I have a higher opinion of men. I will honor my husband. You can talk that way, but not around me." Draw a line in the sand and don't let people cross it. If your buddy is always pointing out hot girls to you, tempting you to lust, explain plainly, "I'm not putting up with that." Don't let someone else pull you down. Set your standards. Express your standards. Then stand strong. It may seem difficult at first, but the more you practice, the more comfortable you'll become. I won't let you talk to me or treat me that way.

Second, you can explain to people, "I'm not going there with you." If others decide to live toxically, you don't have to join them. For example, if you used to have a problem with alcohol and your friend invites you to a keg party where you know you'll be tempted, politely turn down the invitation. Just say no and don't feel pressure to give an explanation. *No* — that one word is a complete sentence.

If the person you're dating pushes you sexually, tell them with an attitude, "No ring, no thing, can't touch this!" Then stand up, start dancing and singing, "If you like it and you want it, put a ring on it!" Seriously, no music video is necessary. Simply and clearly, tell them it's not happening before marriage. Be loving but be firm. Your body belongs to God and you're living for him — period. If you are married and your old flame contacts you on Facebook and invites you to lunch, put up a fence and say, "No, thanks. I'm not going there with you." Don't give in. It's not worth it.

It was a similar boundary that led me to meet Amy. After becoming a Christian in college, I stopped doing many of the normal sinful activities normal college frat boys are known for. When a non-Christian girl made a move my way, tempting me, I had a choice to make. Would I fall into non-Christian activities or take a stand and make my boundary clear? With little hesitation, I explained to her why I wouldn't go along.

She laughed and told me I was weird. Months later, she found me and excitedly told me I should meet a girl who was equally as weird and Jesus-freakish as me. And that's how I met Amy! Six kids and twenty-one years later, we're still Jesus-freakish and weird. Interestingly enough, that former temptress is now a strong Christian and has been an active part of our church. God is good. And so are appropriately placed boundaries.

Cut to the Quick

I'm not a big fan of cats. But I am a big fan of my children, who love cats, so we have two of those not-good-for-much creatures: Binky and Freddy. (Actually, I secretly like cats. I just can't eat a whole one by myself.) Even though cats aren't my favorite animal, I was upset when Binky got hit by a car. Now he has only eight lives left.

Our vet told us that because of the severity of his injuries, our cat would be healthier if we amputated his leg. The lifeless leg now filled with infections would at best slow down our cat, and at worst, the infections could spread, threatening the remaining lives of our family kitty. Now, unfortunately, our cat has only three legs. (I wanted to change his name to Tripod, but the kids wouldn't let me.) But our cat Binky is alive. You see where I'm going with this: sometimes we have to take drastic measures in order to preserve our own relational health.

As harsh as it may sound, hang with me. If you try faithfully to establish healthy boundaries with a toxic person and the person continues to abuse, criticize, threaten, tempt, or harm you, it's time to cut off the toxic relationship. The right thing to do is sever the relationship to protect yourself.

To be crystal clear, I'm not talking about divorcing your spouse. We don't divorce, abandon, or cut off our spouses just because we are having a difficult time. If you are having a tough time in your marriage, don't run into the bedroom shouting, "You're toxic so I'm leaving you!" Instead, call your pastor or a Christian counselor and work on your marriage. Let me say it again, I'm not talking about divorce here.

I'm also not talking about cutting off one of your family members. It must break God's heart how often a parent writes off a child or a sibling stops speaking to another. With the exception of extreme abuse, most problems can be resolved. But every now and then, if a relationship is so toxic that it threatens the spiritual health (or physical safety) of another, then it's time to amputate.

We see several examples of cutting off relationships in the Bible. When Paul and Barnabas had a sharp disagreement, rather than fighting about it, going to court, or gossiping all over town, they decided to go their separate ways (see Acts 15). In the Old Testament, God told his people not to marry people who follow false gods (Deut. 7), and the New Testament tells believers not to be yoked or joined to unbelievers (2 Cor. 6:14).

We should befriend people who don't know Christ — until they begin undermining our faith and hurting us spiritually. Then if we can't redefine the relationship and it becomes increasingly dangerous, we must cut off the relationship. Genesis 39 shows us a great example as Joseph faithfully and loyally served his master, Potiphar. He did anything the family needed, until Potiphar's wife crossed a line and made a move on Joseph. The story says, "She caught him by his cloak and said, 'Come to bed with me!' But he left his cloak in her hand and ran out of the house" (Gen. 39:12). Let's hope he had on his long johns that day. Just saying.

Notice Joseph didn't stick around to share his faith with the seductive wife. He didn't stop and hold hands with her to share a prayer. Instead, he got out of Dodge. He severed, cut off, and ended whatever type of relationship they had. She was gangrene, so he cut off the relationship immediately.

If you're a teenager and someone is sexting you and won't stop, do something dramatic. If you've warned him repeatedly and asked him to quit, then change your number. Tell an adult. Don't put up with that kind of disrespectful abuse. If you are in business with someone who insists on doing something unethical, try to talk her out of it. If she won't budge and threatens to damage your reputation, get out of the partnership. Buy her out. Sell your part. Cut your losses. End the relationship.

If you're married and someone at work flirts with you constantly and you're starting to feel tempted, don't stick around pretending it will get better. If you know deep down you're playing with fire, exit the building. If they don't stop, report them to a supervisor or the human resources department, or ask for a transfer, but don't tolerate it. Sever the relationship so no one gets sick.

If you are dating someone who is a jerk and everyone knows it, break up. Dump him. Drop him. Throw that little fish back in the pond. Do yourself a favor and stop settling. Why would you insult God by settling for someone who is not worthy of you? Once you've tried and tried and tried but failed to detox a toxic friend, it's time to clear out so you can heal.

Last Resort

Before you start blasting people out of your life, let me reiterate an important point. Cutting people off should be a rare and last-resort measure. Based on my experience, ending relationships is more common the younger you are. For example, teens and adults in their twenties are often working to find their identity. As people are still discovering who they are (or who they are not), they might pick up some of the wrong relationships along the way and need to end them.

Ending relationships might also be more common for a new Christian. If you are coming out of a very sinful lifestyle and starting to follow Christ, prayerfully you can help your old friends. Often though, your previous crowd could hurt your new life more than you can help their old life. If that is the case, you might need to redefine some relationships or cut them off completely. When in doubt, Proverbs reminds us to play it safe: "The righteous choose their friends carefully, but the way of the wicked leads them astray" (12:26).

As we mature both spiritually and with age, ending relationships should become more and more uncommon. Although dozens of people have drifted in and out of our lives and we've redefined as many relationships or more, we haven't had to cut out anyone in more than twenty years.

The most important thing to remember is the why. Jesus separated himself and boxed out the Pharisees so that he could know God and minister his love. If you ever have to distance yourself from someone toxic, the only reason is to protect yourself so you can be spiritually strong, know God intimately, and share his love. You must be spiritually healthy if you want to bring God's healing love to a world of sick people.

12

Religion Gone Bad

Tossing Out Moldy Legalism, Spoiled Churches, and Sour Christians

The tendency to turn human judgments into divine commands makes religion one of the most dangerous forces in the world.
—Georgia Harkness

Whenever I'm enjoying a great conversation with someone I just met and they ask what I do for a living, I'm always tempted to lie. So far I never have, but I always think about telling them that I'm an aerospace engineer (astronaut sounds a little far-fetched) or a neurologist (brain surgeon sounds so common), anything other than the truth.

Whenever I reveal that I'm a Christian pastor, the conversation always changes. If the person is a believer, he or she instantly switches into I'm-in-the-club-too spiritual talk: "Praise the Lord, Pastor. Thank you, Jesus!" We might've been discussing pick-up trucks, college football, or three-legged cats, but the moment a fellow believer discovers my profession, they immediately start speaking Christianeze.

However, if the person isn't a Christian, then the moment they find out I'm a pastor, their shields go up faster than those on the USS *Enterprise* in a fleet of Klingons. On a recent flight I sat by a really nice business guy named Steve who couldn't make an escape when he discovered that I'm a pastor, but I could tell he wanted to run — good thing we weren't sitting in an exit row! Defensively, he exclaimed, "Well, I'm not religious!" I nodded and said, "No problem," and tried to return to our discussion of our favorite apps. However, my response must not have been convincing for Steve because he repeated himself and fired an extra warning shot in case I'd missed the first: "I'm not religious, and I can't stand religious people."

Steve's shield firmly in place, I politely asked him to tell me more about the retail business that he was in. Ignoring my question, he glared at me, "Look, I told you that I'm not religious and I don't like religious people!" I then realized that he must be carrying some wound from past experiences with religion and religious people. "I totally understand and respect your opinion," I said, as sympathetically as possible, while praying a silent S.O.S. prayer to God for wisdom. "Tell me more about why you got into the business you're in," I said, hoping to defuse the mounting tension. "I told you," he bellowed, trying to appear in control but clearly exasperated, "I'm not religious, and I can't stand religious people!"

I looked at him for a moment in silence and then decided to tell Steve the truth: "We've got a lot in common then. I'm not religious, and I can't stand religious people either!"

Steve stared at me awkwardly, like a cow watching burgers on a grill. "What do you mean?" he sputtered. "But I thought you were a pastor?"

As best I could, I explained that God didn't send his only Son to earth in order to die for the sake of a new religion. I told Steve that I honestly don't like people who are wrapped up in legalistic religion and that Jesus himself corrected that type of person many times in his ministry on earth. I explained that Jesus came for those who were sick, not those who thought they were well and better than everybody else.

After a long conversation, Steve said, "I like you — you're honest. You are the first nonreligious pastor that I've ever met."

It may be one of the best compliments I've ever received.

Religious Nausea

Contrary to what many believe, Jesus did *not* come to earth to make us religious. He came to set us free. Jesus said that our enemy the devil comes to steal and destroy, but that he came to bring life and life to the fullest (see John 10:10). He said that he didn't come for the self-proclaimed righteous people but for sinners (see Luke 5:32). In its purest sense, Christianity is not intended to be one of the world's major religions, but rather it is supposed to be a relationship with the one, true, living God through his Son, Jesus.

Sadly, the purity of the gospel is often tainted by poisonous people. When people refuse to live by faith, when they're afraid of trusting God and the power of his love, then they usually resort to some form or formula. In fact, religion is defined as any system, set of rules, expectations, or regulations that promises God's acceptance in return for human effort. It may sound right, but it couldn't be more wrong and dangerous. Some scholars even argue that the root of the word *religion* means "return to bondage." Rather than progressing to spiritual freedom, man-made religious rules lead straight to a spiritual prison where people die a lonely godless death.

You can see a strong example of toxic religion in the New Testament. The apostle Paul was in many ways a church planter. He led people to Christ in a region, raised up new Christians as leaders, empowered them to care for a church, then repeated the process in another town. Galatia was one such community where Paul helped start a church. After he had moved on to another region, he was devastated to discover that a group called the Judaizers had followed him into Galatia and started adding their own rules to the gospel of Christ. The Judaizers basically said, "What Paul taught you about Jesus was a good start. But to really be right with God, you need Jesus *and* you need to be circumcised." In other words, they believed you still had to obey the whole Jewish law.

You can only imagine the tension for every uncircumcised male adult. In my role as a pastor, it's difficult enough to convince most men to get baptized, let alone circumcised. (Can you see me at the end of the service addressing the male members of our congregation? "If you'd like to get right with God," I'd begin and then hold up a razor-sharp scalpel — okay, enough said.)

Fighting the Judaizers' false teaching, Paul penned a scathing letter to the church he loved: "I am astonished that you are so quickly deserting the one who called you to live in the grace of Christ and are turning to a different gospel — which is really no gospel at all. Evidently some people are throwing you into confusion and are trying to *pervert the gospel of Christ*" (Gal. 1:6 – 7, emphasis mine). The Greek word translated here as "to pervert" is *metastrepho*. It means "to taint, corrupt, distort, or poison." The Judaizers' additional rules polluted the purity of the gospel with religion.

What Not to Wear

Any time you stumble into toxic religion, you'll likely see two poisonous problems. The first is that religion leads you to focus on the external rather than the internal. Religion requires a behavior-oriented path toward pleasing God. These people, often well-intentioned, focus on an outward expression rather than an inward transformation. Religion is our effort to close the gap between sinful humans and a holy God. Sadly, it reduces the beauty of the gospel to a checklist of do's and don'ts. Rules regulate religion.

Few groups practiced religion with the precision of the Pharisees in Jesus' day. Consider the contrast: as Christians, empowered by God's Spirit, we follow his Ten Commandments. Jesus even reduced the ten down to the most important two: love God and love people.

The Pharisees, on the other hand, memorized and faithfully executed 613 commands! It's like memorizing the installation and operating instructions for your new 3D-HD TV. Astonishingly, the rules-loving Pharisees mostly lived up to those 613 commands. Outwardly, they appeared to be very law-abiding, good people. But inwardly, their hearts were pridefully focused on their superiority and righteousness, not on God or showing his love to others.

When the Pharisees prayed, they wanted to be seen and heard by people as they uttered unnecessarily long and showy prayers to impress the onlookers. When they gave money in the temple, they would hold up their offering for everyone to see, making a show of their generosity and proving once again just how righteous they were. Jesus warned them again and again with shockingly stern words. In Matthew 23:25, he said, "Woe to you, teachers of the law and Pharisees, you hypocrites! You clean the outside of the cup and dish, but inside they are full of greed and self-indulgence." In other words, you wiped off the outside of the container that the rest of us see, but inside it's teeming with every kind of germ and virus. You look good on the outside, but inside — where it counts — your soul is filthy.

God hates the outward show. In fact, in many ways, Life Church was a result of my frustrations with religion. Years ago in my mid-twenties, I had an experience that confirmed my desires to do church in a different way. Guest preaching one Sunday morning at a sister church, I stood and greeted people as they approached the sanctuary. One woman, obviously a first-time visitor to the church, approached apprehensively. While everyone else had on their best suits and dresses and carried five-pound Bibles, this woman's disheveled outfit appeared to be overdue for a good cleaning. Her hair was pulled back loosely, and a few strands hid her eyes as she nervously looked at all the regular attenders around her.

As she approached, I thought to myself, "God, you are going to do something special in her life today." Just then the older man next to me stepped forward and said, "Lady, we wear our best clothes to this church. Is that the best outfit you have?"

She stopped in her tracks, stunned, and then turned away, got into her car, and drove off. I still pray for this woman to this day. God doesn't look at the outside (see 1 Sam. 16:7). Why do religious people focus on what people wear and miss the fact that another person's heart is searching for God?

With this experience in mind, I tell people at our church that I don't care what kind of clothes they have. If you have the best labels, the worst labels, or even crooked labels (remember my Izod fiasco?), come and worship. Our dress code is: please do. Cover the essentials and come to Christ. If you are rich, poor, black, white, yellow, or orange, come to know the truth of Christ. If you've tried to be good all your life or if you've been the worst person you know, come to Christ. God doesn't look at the outside. God judges the heart. Come to the one who loves you just as you are.

Did I mention that I can't stand religious people?

Noxious Gas

Not only does religion focus on the externals rather than the internals but this external emphasis produces an internal pride. Rules-following religious people believe their behavior and beliefs are right and everyone else is wrong. It's like a piece of food that spoils — not only is it nasty and ruined but it emits a noxious smell as well.

Jesus told this story to a religious group proud of their righteous behaviors: "Two men went up to the temple to pray, one a Pharisee and the other a tax collector. The Pharisee stood by himself and prayed: 'God, I thank you that I am not like other people — robbers, evildoers, adulterers — or even like this tax collector. I fast twice a week and give a tenth of all I get'" (Luke 18:10 – 12).

It's interesting that Jesus contrasted a Pharisee and a tax collector. Whereas Pharisees were outwardly religious, tax collectors were the opposite. At the time Jesus walked the earth, people despised tax collectors more than anyone else. Regarded by society as in the same class as murderers, tax collectors regularly stole from the common people. Since they lived in a time without email, letters, or computers, hearing from a tax collector was the only way people found out how much money they owed. Since people couldn't prove whether the collector was lying, he regularly added a little extra to the bill to keep for himself. You can imagine why people hated them so much. A Pharisee wouldn't even allow the hem of his robe to touch a tax collector. And the Pharisee in the temple shouted to everyone, "I'm righteous and thankful I'm not like that low-down, good-for-nothing, immoral tax guy next to me."

Yet even as the Pharisee proclaimed, "Thank God I'm not like this low-class, low-life tax collector over there!" he couldn't see his own poisonous pride. Spiritual pride is almost impossible to see in the mirror. When someone is convinced he is right about religion, anyone who tries to correct him is obviously wrong. Toxic religion puffs up its host. It pollutes and infects those it touches.

One time a guy came to my door to share his faith in Christ. Excited to see a Christian out sharing his faith, I decided to give him some practice. A few minutes into his presentation, I realized that I needed to come clean with him. "I'm actually a committed Christian," I told him, explaining how impressed I was with his witness.

"What church do you go to?" he asked excitedly. Without revealing my pastoral role, I told him I was a part of Life Church.

When he heard the name, his countenance fell. Looking around nervously, he leaned in and whispered, "My pastor says the pastor of Life Church doesn't preach the truth."

I leaned in and whispered back, "Your pastor needs to be circumcised, and I volunteer to do it."

Okay, so I didn't say that. But boy, I wanted to! Why do you think so many non-Christians can't stand Christians? For starters, our spiritual pride often makes it impossible for us to get along with each other. Why should we be any better with anyone else? Some religious Christians are so convinced that their way of doing church is the only way, they discount and denounce every other style or philosophy. In doing so, they unknowingly become inward-looking and sour people. Why in the world would someone without Christ want to join a joyless, cynical, hypercritical, and judgmental group of religious people? Thankfully, Jesus didn't come to make us religious. He brought us the good news of eternal life.

Good News, Bad News

You can be around the church, like I was growing up, and not understand the gospel. Some people have a "head knowledge" of Jesus but not a "heart understanding" of the gospel. They miss his life by about eighteen inches. Rather than knowing about Jesus, we need to know him directly through the gospel.

The gospel offers life-giving, life-transforming power through God's free gift of salvation. In three verses, here's the good news of the gospel summarized clearly: "Therefore no one will be declared righteous in God's sight by the works of the law; rather, through the law we become conscious of our sin. But now apart from the law the righteousness of God has been made known … This righteousness is given through faith in Jesus Christ to all who believe" (Rom. 3:20 – 22). It's the opposite of religion, which is the bad news of rules, burdens, and bondage. The gospel is the good news of grace, freedom, and life.

Paul explains three foundational elements in the message of the gospel. Let's briefly examine all three so that the contrast between the gospel and religion is crystal clear.

1. You cannot earn God's acceptance by observing the law. Religion says you can please God by your religious efforts or works. If you try hard and do more good things than bad, you might qualify for God's acceptance. But Paul demonstrates that's not even close to true. Instead, he taught, "No one will be declared righteous by observing the law." No one includes you and includes me. In other words, even the most religious, hardworking, and faithful person on earth will not be good enough to qualify for heaven. Righteousness by human effort is impossible.

Anything that says otherwise is toxic religion. Yet people, churches, and denominations still impose their pet rules on people, leading them into a false sense of spiritual comfort. A religious person might say proudly, "I don't drink, I don't smoke, I don't chew, and I don't run with girls who do," assuming their behavior makes them righteous. Your behavior will never make you righteous.

This good news frees you from attempting to earn God's favor by your hard work. You can try to be a good person, go to church, raise your kids right, give some money, avoid bad movies, try not to cuss, and you still are not righteous. No one — that includes me and you — can be good enough for God on their own.

2. The purpose of the law is to show you that you need a savior. Paul explained that the law makes us aware of our sinfulness. He said that through the law we become conscious of our sin. Let's be honest, once you know the Ten Commandments, it becomes clear that you've broken several, if not all of them. I know I have. The law shows you that you aren't good enough and that you need help.

Evangelist and author Ray Comfort asks a series of questions to help people see their need for Christ. Here's my version of his questions: Have you ever told a lie? If you say no, you just lied. Of course you have lied. Since you've told a lie, what does that make you? Answer: a liar. Ready for another question? Have you ever put something ahead of God? Again, I'm sure you have. What does that make you? Answer: an idolater. Feel bad about yourself yet? Let's keep going. Have you ever stolen something? I have. If you have taken something that didn't belong to you, what are you? Answer: a thief. Simply put, we are lying, idolatrous, thieving sinners. And the list could go on and on. The law shows us that we aren't good enough. We are sinful people who need a savior. We don't need religion. We need Christ.

3. *Righteousness from God comes by faith in Christ alone.* Paul could not have been more direct. He said, "This righteousness is given through faith in Jesus Christ to all who believe" (Rom. 3:22). Wow! That is the best news you'll hear in your entire life. Enjoy those life-giving words again slowly. "This righteousness is given through faith in Jesus Christ to all who believe." I love the word *all*.

How about a few more questions? Does "all" include doubters, adulterers, or those who battle with lust? Of course. Does "all" include those who cuss, cheat, and lose their temper each time they play golf? You bet it does. How about all the people who've been hurt by religion, damaged by rules, and poisoned by toxic churches? Obviously, yes! Anyone and everyone who puts their faith in Christ will be made righteous by Christ. There's no better news imaginable!

Robed in Glory

When I was an associate pastor at a United Methodist church in my early twenties, I got to sit at the front of the church on one of four thrones. Yes, that's right, I said thrones. Technically, I suppose they were just fancy, oversized wooden chairs with big padded cushions, but to me, they looked like thrones. To this day I'm not sure why, but the thrones were not the same size. Two of them were king-sized thrones and reserved for the senior pastor and his right-hand man, and two were smaller, less important looking, junior-sized thrones. Being the rookie and youngest pastor, you can guess which throne I sat on.

Not only did the senior pastor and two other ministers sit before the whole church in throne-like chairs as everyone looked our way, but we also wore robes on Sundays. As if my somewhat-smaller throne weren't enough to keep me humble, the robes also revealed rank. The ordained pastors who sat on the larger thrones donned majestic robes complete with two vertical stripes displayed for all to see. My robe on the other hand looked like a forty-year-old choir robe that someone wore to play football in the mud. It was stained and stripeless, proclaiming to everyone that I was not a full-blown pastor but still just a hopeful trainee.

One Sunday, my pastor, Nick Harris, preached a powerful sermon about justification by faith. He explained passionately how Christians are made right with God by faith in Christ alone. I sat faithfully on my junior throne taking notes and saying "amen" at the appropriate times, helping my mentor and pastor along. Midway through his message, since I had my legs crossed under the robe, one leg started to fall asleep. Rather than adjusting it to get the blood flowing again, I thought I'd just let it fall asleep. I thought, "Why not?" and kind of amused myself. (I know, maybe that's evidence of why I sat on the smaller throne and didn't have stripes.) Several minutes later, my leg tingled all the way up to my gluteus maximus. Smiling to myself that I'd all but killed one of my legs, I loudly proclaimed, "Amen!" at the first opportunity.

That's when, out of the blue, Pastor Nick did something that he'd never done before or since. In the middle of his sermon, he looked at me and said, "Craig, stand up for a minute."

What! Oh no! I can't stand up. Half my body is in a coma. What am I going to do?

Panicked, I froze like a statue.

"Craig," Nick urged, gently but somewhat more forcefully, "please stand up."

That's when I tried to stand. The moment I put weight on my dead leg, I started to fall toward the prayer rail by the altar area. Nick grabbed me with a look that suggested I'd been drinking the communion wine between services. He stood me up straight as I put all my weight on my good leg, with both hidden by my dingy robe. Thank God for Methodist robes!

Nick asked me in front of the whole church, "Is your robe a *nice* robe?"

I was uncertain of how to respond, but he coached me with his eyes, showing me that he was looking for the truth.

"Um, not really," I said, unclear where he was going with this.

"Not really?" Nick boomed. "It's horrible! Your robe is old, musty, and pathetic."

(So I wasn't the only one who noticed.)

"What do you think about my robe? Is it nice?" he asked, soliciting my positive response. Supporting my answer, Nick continued, "Yes, it is. My robe is clean, beautiful, and perfect in every way." That's when his spontaneous illustration started to take a life of its own.

My pastor asked me to take off my robe and exchange it for his. With great affection, Nick put his spotless, superior robe on me as my ratty, old robe fell to the side. Suddenly, I felt tremendously humbled knowing that I was wearing a robe that I didn't earn and certainly didn't deserve.

Nick explained with great emotion that on our own, we are all filthy, dead in our own sin. But when Christ came, he put his robe of righteousness over our sin. Now, because of our faith in Christ, when God looks at us, he doesn't see our sin. Our Father in heaven sees only the righteousness of Christ. All our sins are covered. In God's eyes, we are pure.

Relationship Eats Religion for Breakfast

Remember the story Jesus told about the Pharisee and the tax collector? The self-righteous religious Pharisee stood boldly in the synagogue and proclaimed, "Look how righteous I am! I do all these good things. Thank God I'm not like that no-good tax collector." Jesus never stood for that kind of religious pride. To make his point, Jesus continued his story: "But the tax collector stood at a distance. He would not even look up to heaven, but beat his breast and said, 'God, have mercy on me, a sinner'" (Luke 18:13). Instead of having pride in himself, this repentant tax collector cried out to God for mercy.

Certainly Jesus stunned his listeners with such an unexpected twist: "I tell you that this man, rather than the other, went home justified before God. For all those who exalt themselves will be humbled, and those who humble themselves will be exalted" (Luke 18:14). In essence, Christ took his robes of righteousness and covered the tax collector's sins, just as he does with yours and mine today.

Toxic religion tries to add extra buttons, patches, and badges to the perfect and completed garment of Christ's righteousness. Religion is Christ plus anything. In Galatia, some thought it was Christ plus circumcision. In our world, it might be Christ plus church membership. Or Christ plus tithing. Or Christ plus "the right" doctrine or theology. But the gospel is Christ plus *nothing*. The final work of Christ on the cross is everything we need. To be made right with God, we only believe in his Son. By faith we enter a relationship with God through his risen Son, Jesus.

Contrast toxic religion with the pure gospel. Religion is all about what I do. The gospel is all about what Jesus has done. Religion is about me. The gospel is about Jesus. Religion highlights my efforts to do what is right. The gospel highlights what Christ has already done. Religion lures me to believe that if I obey God, he will love me. But the gospel shows me that because God loves me, I get to obey him. Religion puts the burden on us. We have to do what is right. A relationship with Christ puts the burden on him. And because of what he did for us, we get to do what is right. Instead of an obligation, our right living is a response to his gift.

Giving Christ our whole lives is the only reasonable response to such love. There's nothing more we need to do. *Nothing*.

Clean and Sober

*Religion that God our Father accepts as pure and faultless
is this: to look after orphans and widows in their distress
and to keep oneself from being polluted by the world.*
—James 1:27

Congratulations on making it all the way through this book. If you've
read cover to cover, you've done better than I often do. I can't count the
number of books that I have started, highlighting and underlining my
favorite parts, only to stall out three chapters in and leave the partly
read book buried in a drawer right beside a pile of my other good
intentions. (If you skipped ahead to the conclusion like my wife often

does, I'm not talking about you. Subtract ten points from your score if you're a skipper!) On the other hand, if you've read prayerfully with an open heart before God, I wholeheartedly believe that our heavenly Father desires to do something special in your life.

But here's the reality of your situation. This can be another book you read about how to have a stronger faith and a closer walk with the Lord, blah, blah, blah. In fact, you may have already come up with all sorts of great excuses as to why the teaching from God's Word between these pages doesn't apply to you. Like the Pharisee's public prayer of thanksgiving that he wasn't like the tax collector and other riffraff, you may be priding yourself on already knowing all that you've read here. You may feel a bit smug that you already have this God stuff down pat. You're sure that it will help other people and grateful that you don't need to make any changes in your life like they do.

Or perhaps you haven't been the churchgoing, God-believing type of person. Reading all the way through a Christian book might have been a bit of a stretch for you. You might feel tempted to write off all this Bible stuff as sentimental self-help at best and a crutch for the weak-willed at worst.

Or, whether you're a committed Christian, a nominal one, or someone seeking truth, reading this book might be the catalyst that ignites you to change, to finally come clean and admit that you want this time to be different. You desperately want to live a purer life, a holier life, a life in pursuit of this heavenly Father who lavishes you with his love, a life spent walking in the footsteps of Christ, laying down your life for others, living out of a joyful purpose that's more fulfilling than anything this world can offer.

So let's cut to the chase. It's decision time. What do you want to do? Do you want to finish the remaining few pages, check this book off your list, and get back to life as it was? Or do you crave something more, something different, something better? Do you truly want God to reveal to you the pollutants, toxins, and poisons coming at you from every direction? Do you want him to cleanse you and replace the poison with supernatural peace, compassion, and joy?

The choice is yours. You can cover up the spiritual trash that's accumulated in your life or you can do something courageous and come clean from your past mistakes and look ahead to something better. If you decide you want something different, let me warn you. You have an enemy poised to stop you dead in your tracks. Be forewarned: it may be harder to change old habits than ever before. Clean living is a sobering prospect.

Excuses, Excuses

The problem, you see, is that as soon as you decide to be different, your enemy gives you excuses to stay the same. The moment you make a decision, you begin second-guessing that decision because the more you think about it, the more your goal really doesn't seem worth the effort. Poisoned by complacency and addicted to mediocrity, we immediately start talking ourselves out of pursuing what we desire the most. Before we know it, our good intentions go by the wayside like New Year's resolutions fading in February.

Why is it so hard to keep our well-intentioned goals? I believe it's because most of us have good intentions rather than God intentions, and there is a tremendous difference. Good intentions center around us. We say, "Here's what I would like to be different about my life." Good intentions are me-centered. God intentions, on the other hand, are centered on what our Father wants for us. Our intentions tend to focus on what we think we want, but God intentions focus on what he knows we need. Instead of relying on our own abilities, our own strength, our own white-knuckled resolve, if we've got God intentions, we fully rely on God's power to do what he wants us to do. And his power is infinitely stronger than our strongest excuse.

Why Power, Not Will Power

So if we want God to finish what he started in us, how can we quit making excuses? How can we let go of our good intentions to change and instead embrace God intentions? I believe the answer lies in how we answer a couple of questions. First, after reading this book, what does God want to be different in your life? Yep, you heard me. What does God, the Creator of the universe who loves you and has great plans for you, want to change in your way of living? I challenge you to prayerfully consider this question, to ask God with honesty and sincerity. What God wants may be the very same thing that you want, but when you attribute the idea to God rather than yourself, it's going to change the way you approach change.

Maybe God wants to make you more self-aware. As you discover your strengths and weaknesses, God might be stirring you to start a ministry, launch a business, or write your own book. Or perhaps God wants to renew your mind, replacing toxic lies with timeless truths. You've been gripped with fear, and its poison has kept you from obeying what God put on your heart. Perhaps you've got some relationships that fall into the "bad company" category. God showed you clearly that you should make some changes, but you're reluctant, not wanting to hurt someone's feelings or stir up controversy. Be honest. What is God showing you that should be different about your life?

Once you have an idea of what it is God's calling you to do differently, then consider the other important question you must ask: *why* does God want this to be different in your life? Why would he want you to make certain changes at this time? Connecting the dots between the "what he's asking" and the "why he's asking" is crucial if you want to experience lasting, life-giving change. When you connect the spiritual why with the what, you find spiritual power and divine motivation to accomplish the change.

Let's consider a couple of examples. Maybe when you prayerfully consider what God wants you to change in your life, you believe he wants you to stop watching certain shows (or reading certain books, or surfing certain sites, or listening to certain music). Why does God want you to curb your media intake? Well, because that stuff is bad, right?

No, that's you answering the why, not God! His answer is based on the fact that your body is the temple of the Holy Spirit. He wants you to have the mind of Christ. He wants you to live like Christ lived, love like Christ loved, and do what Christ did. But when you poison your mind it limits your living. God wants something better for you.

Or maybe after asking God what he wants to change in your life, you find that he really wants you to stop believing the lie that more things equals a better life. God is stirring you to simplify, to get out of debt. Why does God want this for you? Because materialism is bad and debt is worse? No, that's your idea.

God wants you free from serving the lower things of this world. God desires that you know the true joy of serving only him, not created things. God wants you free! Free from lusting after this world and craving things that won't last. Free from the bondage of debt. God wants to give you something better than this world has to offer.

When you connect the spiritual why with the what, suddenly all the excuses that used to keep you away start to diminish. You find yourself motivated by the one who asked you to do it and for his glory. When you know what God wants for you, when you agree and accept what he's calling you to pursue, then there's no excuse on earth that can keep it from happening.

You Talkin' to Me?

Consider a story from the Old Testament, a great example of our human excuses and God's response to them. God called Moses to help deliver the Israelites from the bondage of slavery to the Egyptians. The people had been crying out for deliverance, so God chose a man to lead the charge. And Moses was immediately out of his comfort zone. My experience confirms what we see here: when God asks us to do something, it's not usually something we can accomplish easily — in fact, it may seem impossible to us — because if we could accomplish it easily, then we wouldn't need God.

So, basically, God said, "Moses, you're my guy."

Moses said, "Uh, sorry, God. I'm not your guy." Before you could toast a marshmallow on a burning bush, Moses immediately started in with the excuses. "Moses said to the LORD, 'Pardon your servant, Lord. I have never been eloquent, neither in the past nor since you have spoken to your servant. I am slow of speech and tongue'" (Ex. 4:10). Basically, he said, "Thanks but no thanks, God. Nice of you to ask, but I have this thing about public speaking. I'm not good enough to talk about sheep-tending at Toastmasters, let alone to make the speech of a lifetime in front of Pharaoh."

Moses immediately focused on his inabilities rather than God's unlimited abilities. He looked at his limited power rather than God's unlimited power. You might be tempted to do the same thing. When God shows you something that he wants you to change, you might hesitate and think, "I can't do that." But God will do the same thing to you that he did to Moses — get right up in his business: "The LORD said to him, 'Who gave human beings their mouths? Who makes them deaf or mute? Who gives them sight or makes them blind? Is it not I, the LORD?'" (Ex. 4:11). In other words, "Am I not the one who created you, Moses? Could it be that I know what you're capable of better than you do? If I'm going to ask you to do something, don't you think that since I'm on your side, I'm going to help you get it done?"

When God shows you what he wants you to change, don't you think he's going to help you get it done? Don't you know that he put this book in your hands at this particular time in your life for a reason?

Returning to our buddy Moses, we find that God shared some tough love. Basically, he told Moses to stop whining and start trusting: "Now go; I will help you speak and will teach you what to say" (Ex. 4:12). God was saying to Moses, "Go on, just do what you can do, the next thing. I've told you what to do, so quit thinking about it and making excuses and just go do it!"

The Right Time

If you're reading this and you know what God wants you to do, then put this book down and go do it! Seriously. Someone said, "Delayed obedience is disobedience." Don't you dare delay! If God has shown you how he wants you to live differently, if he's revealed what you need to give up or what you need to embrace, then do not disobey him by procrastinating and waiting until "the time is right." The time is right, now. The time is right now!

Unless God gives you a timetable, then he's talking about *right now*. It's like when Amy or I ask one of our kids to go get something for us in another room. "I'll do it later, Dad," they say. "Wait until I finish this level of Angry Birds and I'll get it for you then." And I'm thinking, "How 'bout we play a little Angry Parents? I mean right now, not in a minute or two when you don't have anything better to do!"

If God wants you to quit smoking and you're waiting on him to take your desire away, but you're still lighting up one after another, then I'll just say it — you're crazy! Not for smoking — we all have our vices — but for not doing your part. Throw the cigarettes away. Talk to your doctor, get help, join a group, get rid of the smokes. Now! If you know you need to give up a toxic relationship at work but you're waiting for God to move this person to another department so you won't risk hurting their feelings, then you're crazy too. You have to do what you can do, whether it's having a hard conversation and confronting this person or steering clear and asking to be transferred yourself.

If you believe God wants to give you wholesome relationships to replace your toxic ones, act on what he shows you. If you sense that he wants you to befriend a person in your book group, then pick up the phone and call. Don't wait to get stuck in an elevator together; take the initiative and do the next thing. If God wants something to be different in your life, then you must do what you know to do, and do it now!

God concluded his message to Moses by saying, "Go, and when you go I will help you and teach you." He implied that Moses must do his part and trust God to do the rest. God initiates and we respond.

Think about what could be different in your life and in the lives of those around you if you quit making excuses, if you lived with God intentions and let go of your own agenda. If you truly want to live a cleaner, purer life, a more Christ-centered, Spirit-filled life, then it's time to take the next steps that you know to take. Do what you can do and trust God to do what you can't.

My prayer is that right now, God is speaking to your heart and making his message loud and clear.

Can you hear him?

Now, go — in his strength and by his power — just do it!

Godspeed!

Acknowledgments

Thank you to all my friends who offered support, encouragement, and assistance with this book. I'm especially thankful for:

Dudley Delffs. You do with words what LeBron James does with a basketball. I'm your number one fan (in a non-stalker type of way).

Tom Dean, Cindy Lambert, and Brian Phipps, and the whole team at Zondervan. I love your commitment to excellence and to Christ-centered publishing.

Tom Winters. Thanks for your wisdom on book projects and beyond. You are more than an agent. You are also a trusted friend.

Brannon Golden. Thank you for your work early on in the project. Your family is a huge blessing to our church and to me.

Ali Burleson. You are the master final editor. Plus, you're one
    cool chick.

Lori Tapp. Thank you for keeping me sane at the office. You
    are a gift.

Catie, Mandy, Anna, Sam, Stephen, and Joy. Your love for our
    Savior blesses me more than you'll ever know. I'm so proud
    of you.

Amy. You are my "Christian babe." I praise God for bringing
    us together.